GOD'S CONMAN

The Reverend James Currie, 1921–1987

GOD'S CONMAN
The Life and Work of
The Reverend James Currie

WILLIAM COFFEY

Foreword by Lord Elgin
Lord High Commissioner of the General Assembly
of the Church of Scotland, 1980–1981

LOCHAR PUBLISHING   MOFFAT · SCOTLAND

Published by Lochar Publishing Ltd
          Bankhead
          Annan Water
          MOFFAT DG10 9LS

British Library Cataloguing in Publication Data
Coffey, William. 1951–
   God's conman.
   1. Church of Scotland. Currie, James.
   1930–1987
   I. Title
   285'.2'0924

   ISBN 0-948403-10-1

Photoset in 10½ on 12½ Times by Hewer Text, Edinburgh and
printed by A Wheaton & Co. Exeter.

To Peggy
The remarkable wife of a remarkable man

CONTENTS

by Lord Elgin

In *God's Conman*, The Revd James Currie and William Coffey together give us a traveller's tale which, steadily, becomes a progress. 'A Journey of a Lifetime', the travel agent cries, but there the similarity stops. That sort of journey is for curiosity, Currie's journey was for life – to be more accurate – lives. Door upon door opened to people, many showed shock at the sight of him, but the shock turned to attraction, and many thereafter could not bear to lose sight of him.

I was unfortunate enough not to have met James until after he had left Pollok, so I never felt the single-minded, all-out minister of Renton or Pollok. For me, the wonderful parish days had gone; I met, head-on, the whirlwind world of Currie. What I most enjoyed about the book was to be taken, step by fruitful step, through the stages of childhood and learning, the very tender flowering of self-confidence and the solid gains of achievement on the farm, playing rugby and teaching children. Because he knew he could succeed at all these things, so was he the better able to fulfil his ministry.

I have suggested that I met him first in the full flood of his second, reputedly more restrained, life – it was planned thus, but I got the 'flu. As chairman of the Dunfermline United Burns Club, I lay fuming in bed while my wife escorted the large clergyman up to the meeting. Tediously, the hours passed. I wondered what was up. I had always tethered the meeting to stop at midnight, and now it was long past. When, at last, I heard the front door open, and the babble of sound arise, I sensed what had happened. James had just gone rapturously on – Robert Burns had, with similar feelings, surely returned to the City Hotel, Dunfermline, and the members of the club had recaptured their link with their Creator, for all it was misty with tears and sore on their ribs. That night they learned the meaning of Immortality!

A year later, I was asked by the General Assembly to help in raising funds for the building of churches in the ever-increasing wonderland of the new towns of Scotland. The appeal was specifically set to find donations of £1000 and upwards. It was determined to use the device of a musical evening. Ultimately, the people who helped me were known as 'Elgin's Flying Chorus', and James was a most honoured member. One night, I took with me the great Sword of State of King Robert Bruce. James asked if he could touch it. Then he took it in his hands. Such hands – at times hugely safe and capable, then dancing lightly as they outlined the shape of Raquel Welch, but really they were shepherd's hands – you could see them lock on to a sheep and hold it surely until calm might come and the dipping or shearing competently done.

As his biographer so rightly says, James was forever torn between the plough and the pulpit, with the result that there was ever a tremendous mental strain. What I do remember was James telling me that without Arran and its special relaxation he could not have kept up the pace on the mainland. Even as the word 'A-a-a-rran' came from his lips, his eyes were alight with love. Conflict there may have been, but both callings were safe in his perfect grasp.

The story makes not a little of the divergencies of view between himself and other ministers – indeed, at times, the authority of the Church itself. I never felt that James stepped wittingly over the boundaries to cause offence, rather, he had picked up the wrong map. His map was of the world at the time of Christ, a great deal was unknown and heathen. To him, Christ's instructions were clear – he was to go out into the world. This book tells you how he did it, and who he met.

However, to enjoy it, you must be fit yourself. In the very reading you will dash hither and thither, answer the telephone at all hours, drink a cup of tea with one hand and pick up an electric razor with the other, prepare to baptise twenty children, agree to speak in Winnipeg on Tuesday and lunch in Glasgow the following day, attend your Presbytery that afternoon and arrange to be collected by the Police for their Burns Supper in the evening. Currie made a long time out of a week, but to me he was so very near my forebear in the 16th century Church – Master Robert Bruce. Bruce had not entered the Church easily. He first prospered at quite another calling, until his conscience was upset. He described it thus: 'God made me first a Christian before He made me a Minister'. Then, in a famous sermon, he spoke these words, 'Unless you hear Christ in a familiar and homely language, you cannot understand; and unless you understand, it is not possible for you to believe.'

As I am a family traditionalist, I used to love hearing James Currie use this same style, and I believe that it has not lost its pertinence over three-and-a-half centuries, and that is why this book will touch your heart.

At the age of thirteen, James Currie walked through the rose garden
with the headmaster of his school and decided to become a minister.
They had not discussed his career. 'It was just God's plan,' James said.
It brought him joy and despair. It was tested to the point of breaking,
but it held, and created Scotland's most charismatic minister – a man
of the people.

He became a 'personality', yet was haunted by shyness. When he
attended university he took sandwiches and ate them locked in the
lavatory. He could not believe his fellow students would want to hear
anything he had to say and feared they would laugh at him. This lack
of confidence never left him.

His passion for Glasgow Rangers and association with the Orange
Order led him to be labelled a bigot, yet he was criticised by Kirk
authorities for ministering to Roman Catholics. He could not refuse a
request for assistance: 'What am I to do – leave the people Godless?'
His motive was often mistaken for arrogance, but, he said, 'Christ had
to carry a cross.'

If there was one thing James Currie liked more than laughing it was
making others laugh. He knew grief and its antidote. He cried easily,
openly and unashamedly. More often, he laughed. Children adored
him, and he loved being with them, yet he confessed that he spent
little time with his three sons as they grew up: 'I was too busy.'

His best work was done when he was at St James Church, Pollok,
Glasgow. He had almost three thousand church members and about
ten thousand regular attenders. He maintained there was no secret to
this success. It was all due to the parish system: caring for the needs of
everyone in the parish and taking the church to those people.

James Currie was born at Drumadoon Farm, Blackwaterfoot,
Arran. When his father died, he took over the tenancy and later
bought the farm. It was a financial millstone, 'good money after bad',
but he kept it as a memorial to the father he adored. While he was
running the farm and acting as minister to ten thousand, he suffered a
heart attack and reluctantly moved to the smaller parish of Dunlop

where he 'regarded every day as a bonus'. Seventeen years later, after a day working in his fields in Arran and an evening preaching in his pulpit in Ayrshire, he died, from a heart attack.

It is ironic that the value of a man's life is reflected by the people who attend his funeral service. The service for James Currie was broadcast live on Radio Westsound from his own kirk. The church was full and people stood in the graveyard listening to the proceedings over loudspeakers. Police officers who directed traffic estimated that there were one thousand mourners. Television cameras filmed the dignitaries, but there were folk from all walks of life. They were there because they knew James Currie and, of course, because he knew them. Each and every one of them, and many, many more he had helped and befriended and regarded as a dignitary.

I must take the opportunity to apologise for the omission of those whose words and deeds deserve recognition. There simply was not sufficient time or space to encompass the many spheres of life touched by James Currie. I would also like to thank everyone approached for their full and selfless co-operation. Many of the stories recorded in these pages are highly personal, and I was conscious by asking people to relate them I was intruding into their private affairs and rekindling emotional experiences. I did not attempt to persuade anyone to talk to me, but no one said 'No'. Without exception, they wanted to help 'for James'. Failures and inadequacies are mine: any degree of success belongs to those members of Currie's broad church.

I must also pay unstinting thanks to James Currie's family for their kindness, honesty and co-operation in what were a demanding and apparently never-ending series of interviews. Peggy particularly, despite a succession of illnesses which have prohibited her from working since James's death, was not only a supreme source of information but a stout support when my resolve and confidence was failing. She is the remarkable woman behind a remarkable man. She wanted this book written not as a record of her husband's life but of his life's work. She hopes that it will make people think, and reappraise the value of the parish system. Those who know Peggy Currie will tell you that she too is a servant of God.

This book is the extraordinary story of a man who regarded himself as 'an ordinary guy.'

CHAPTER ONE

West Pilton toll

James Currie's ministry ended before it began. And before it began he tried all that was humanly possible to avoid it.

It started during the Second World War, in West Pilton, Edinburgh, a far cry from the farm on Arran where he was born and brought up. West Pilton was an area cleft into three: street after street of tenements for large families from the slum clearances of Leith; modest, owner-occupied flats and houses; and the comfortable bungalows of the well-to-do.

The membership of the kirk there was divided proportionately, each group keeping itself very much to itself. To James Currie, the kirk's thirteenth assistant minister in a relatively short period, the divisions seemed like chasms. He was fresh from the Iona Community where his belief in unity had been strengthened. The Community was living proof that when barriers were swept aside and all worked as one, nothing was unobtainable. James's immediate goal in West Pilton was to bring everyone together, not only under the roof of the kirk on Sunday but in their everyday life.

He could not have set himself a more demanding task. Wealth set the people of the parish poles apart. In figures, the gulf was not wide. In real terms, however, some families could afford a car and holidays while others could not give their children enough to eat.

The minister at the church, the Revd Allan Easton was a highly-respected member of the establishment, a noted theologian who devoted much of his time to writing books which have stood the test of time. Allan Easton must have seen the potential in James, a big, raw farmer's son. His instructions were simple: 'Visit the sick, visit the poor, visit the people in prison. Go to see those who need you,' and left the young assistant to carry out these demanding tasks.

Hitler's war machine was wreaking havoc across Europe. It added another visit to the list: James had to call on a family who had lost a father or son – or both.

James had reluctantly admitted to himself that he must spend his life in the ministry. But only after years of soul-searching. He really

13

wanted to be a farmer, like his father and his father's father. Yet each time he believed he had reached that conclusion he would be thrust back towards the Church. The plough or the pulpit? Whichever he chose he yearned for the other.

So it was in West Pilton, but he accepted that the longing for the land, the security of his family, and the love of Peggy, his fiancée there, were sacrifices he had to make. He was almost unbearably shy, naïve, and frightened, but he was the arm of God and the people had to draw from his faith when their own was failing them. He felt he could show no weakness.

His first 'home' in Edinburgh was at Acheson House, a Church of Scotland residence in the Canongate, but while on his rounds in the parish he heard there was accommodation available in West Pilton. Hurriedly he made his way to the door of Mrs Fraser, a widow, at 89 Crewe Road West. In his best clerical voice James enquired about the room. Mrs Fraser was not impressed.

'So you're him, are you?' Sniff. 'Well, you look all right.' Sniff. 'Maybe I'll take you. I'll give you a chance anyway. Any nonsense though and you're oot the door.' Sniff.

There was no 'nonsense' and James was soon settled in comfortably and treated like a son. Mrs Fraser's own two boys were fighting in the war, Jimmy in the Army and Bill in the Royal Air Force. Mrs Fraser gave him the love and understanding that he always found so vital.

James threw himself into his work. The population of his parish was 10 000, and he regarded everyone as a possible church member. During those harsh, bleak days his faith was a tremendous comfort and he wanted others to grasp that lifeline. Weekdays were a constant succession of visits: not to preach but to meet the people and let them get to know him. One day Allan Easton, with a twinkle in his eye, asked James to call on two women and try to persuade them to come to church. 'They were curious, brassy women,' said James, 'and I'd never seen their likes before. They were surprised to see me, but they were polite. It was months later somebody told me I should not be going into that kind of house. They were prostitutes.'

It is a popular misconception that a minister does not 'work'. He reports for duty twice on a Sunday, blethers for a bit, sings the hymns and that's it for another week. There are the occasional weddings and funerals, but he never gets his hands dirty or sits behind a desk from nine till five coping with the pressures of business. Somehow, he manages to put in his week popping into houses and drinking tea.

In fact, nothing could be further from the truth. A minister's hours are long and taxing physically, mentally and spiritually. James worked six days a week, fourteen hours a day, and it bore fruit. He was very popular with the children, and that is always popular with the parents. The Sunday School was thriving. Youths were beginning to take a keen interest in the Bible Class. The membership of the church was growing. James no longer felt like a stranger on the streets. God's plan was evolving, but it was about to take a peculiar twist . . .

Allan Easton was deeply involved in writing a book, *Now's the Day*, and it was demanding a great deal of his time. The way the people of the parish were responding to the assistant appeared to be a blessing. He felt he could leave much of the work to James. But responsibility weighed heavily on the young man's shoulders. The more successful he was in building up the membership of the church and its organisation the more work he created for himself. And the busier he became the more he thought of Arran, the farm, his family and Peggy. His faith was secure, but he doubted himself. He felt he was trapped in a circle which was getting smaller and threatening to strangle him.

As the summer of 1947 drew closer James looked forward to going back to the Iona Community to take charge of youth camps. Once there he would be among friends and mentors. The sea winds would blow away his worries and physical labour would strengthen body and spirit. James heard from some of the ministers he had worked with at the Community. They had been asked to go back. He had not been chosen. It was a bitter blow.

James Currie was a man who needed heroes, and particularly encouragement from those heroes. The Revd George MacLeod, now Lord MacLeod of Fuinary, was a hero. The founder of the Community, his work, and his style of ministry, was James's goal. When he was not asked to return to Iona, he was desolate. He wasn't good enough. He had let George MacLeod down. Self-doubt flooded back. And his unhappiness mounted.

James Currie is remembered by those who heard him preach or hold forth at speaking engagements as the ebullient, assured professional, which indeed he was. But those who *knew* him saw the uncertainty and shyness which haunted him. At university, he ate his lunchtime sandwiches locked in the lavatory because he was afraid to talk to his fellow students. 'They were so clever. I was afraid they would laugh at anything I had to say.' That side of his personality never changed. He simply fought to control it. But when he was in deep despair, he reverted to solitude. He did it until the year he died. He did it in 1947.

15

That summer he prayed earnestly for reassurance, for some sign that he was not a failure. All his work, his successes wrought from two and a half years of endeavour seemed to count for nought. He multiplied his doubts in his vivid imagination, dwelling on the finer points of his peers and writing down his own failings. He lost perspective. Humility is an admirable quality, but once out of control it devours confidence leaving a man impotent. And a man who does not believe in himself does not expect others to believe in him.

James's solace at that time was the warmth and friendship he received from Mrs Fraser. But Bill returned from the RAF, wounded, drained, and, it appeared to James, resentful that a stranger should be demanding to much of his mother's affection. He never dared to discuss these assumptions. It appeared to him that he could do little right.

The country was on its knees economically, its wealth channelled into weapons of death, its lifeblood spilled on foreign soil. James was a conscientious objector, ridiculed by some as a coward. His job cards were largely misery, sickness and death. When his onerous duties were at their peak, he was offered a welcome deflection. He was asked to speak at the annual general meeting of the church at Applegarth, Dumfries. He accepted gratefully, and, almost as an afterthought asked Allan Easton's permission. The minister told him in no uncertain terms that he could not be spared, and chastised his assistant for spending too much time away from the parish. In thirty months James had been home five times.

The Church is not just a vocation, a lifestyle or a job. It is all three and more. To desert it is worse than the darkest disillusionment or the bitterest divorce. The defector must decry all that was once dear to him, or denounce himself. The decision to leave it should come only after much soul-searching. But James Currie deserted the Kirk on the spur of the moment.

When he was barred from visiting Applegarth he went to his room and packed his clothes into two suitcases. He said goodbye to no one, not even his beloved Mrs Fraser. But as he took off his clerical collar and packed it away he felt a welcome relief, almost elation. His life was in tatters. He was an abysmal failure who felt he had lived a lie. He had striven for what he believed in most, followed his deepest beliefs, and now he was betraying them all. yet as he boarded the train on the first leg of his journey back to Arran he was simply glad to be free of his burden.

16

When he arrived home he said simply: 'I'm here. I'm not going back. Don't ask me. Just don't ask me.' And no one did.

What could explain such irrational behaviour? How could such minor setbacks have such major effects? Why did a man born to be a minister desert the Church?

James Currie had suffered a nervous breakdown.

CHAPTER TWO

Servant of God

Time is a great healer.

Twelve years later, James Currie was happy at Millburn Church, Renton, Dunbartonshire, and the members of its congregation were happy with him. He had taken on a parish which had 237 members, and of them one hundred had 'either died and gone to heaven or were spiritually dead.' The church's finances were in dire straits. The manse had no electricity and the kirk was badly in need of repair.

In five years Currie had changed all of that. Millburn was rejuvenated. The honest folk in the Vale of Leven responded to his down-to-earth approach, and the church's membership swelled to 1350. The kirk building was refurbished, a new hall constructed, and the manse turned into a comfortable home. James knew he was on the verge of something extra special. And he was not the only one.

A group of strangers sat in the pews of Millburn one Sunday to listen to him preaching. Later that week he was approached and asked if he would become collegiate minister at St James's, Pollok, a church in one of Glasgow's new, sprawling housing schemes. He was flattered, and the prospect excited him, but he did not for one minute seriously consider taking up the offer.

He was reaping the rewards of his hard labour. By this time he was married with three young sons, James, Charles and Iain. He had made many good friends. He was happy and fulfilled at home and at work, the ambitions of any man. But he was not any man, he was a servant of God, and could not ignore His plans.

No member of the Currie household wanted to leave Renton, but leave it they did. And that was the beginning of the most remarkable ministry in Scotland in living memory.

The Revd Clarence Finlayson, the minister of St James's, was a soul mate of James Currie. He believed in the parish system – the Church should serve the needs of every household within its boundary. Its primary purpose was the worship of God and the spreading of His word. The way to do this was to provide help, any kind of help, wherever and whenever it was required. The new partnership set up shop not only as spiritual mentors but social workers, agony aunts, probation officers, furniture removers and baby-sitters!

When Clarence moved to a kirk in Edinburgh, James continued the work with the aid of a number of ministers, assistants and deaconesses. He said there was no magic formula, no secret of success. Whatever the reasons, and I will attempt to explain them later. By 1970, 10 000 folk were regular attenders at St James's and its membership had risen to 3000. Services were broadcast from the kirk so often that the elders were on first name terms with cameramen.

Currie's name was known throughout the land. His face was seen frequently on television and in newspapers. He was taking parties on pilgrimages to the Holy Land. His name was mentioned frequently as a certain candidate for Moderator of the General Assembly of the Church of Scotland. He never actively sought this accolade, but he would have welcomed it. The truth is, he was never in with a chance. He made too many enemies in high places.

He sought to lead by example and this necessitated a high profile. He saw his role as a simple one: he was a servant of God. When asked to officiate at a ceremony he had but one yardstick: would Jesus do this? If the answer was yes, he did it and was often castigated for it.

'What else could I do?' he asked. 'If people came to me when other ministers had, for their own reasons, rejected requests, was I to fail them? That's not the purpose of the Church. Do we really mean to leave people Godless?'

So Currie was an Orangeman, a freemason, a Rangers bigot. A glory-hunter who was such an egotist he was bigger than the Church itself.

In fact, he helped members of the Orange Order and preached at their services. He was not a member of the Order. He spoke at freemasons' meetings, always ending with a prayer. He was not a freemason. He loved Glasgow Rangers Football Club and was chaplain to the supporters' federation, but was such a bigot that he wanted Rangers to sign Celtic's Roman Catholic midfield player Paul McStay. The 'big-head' dared to cross boundaries when he thought Christ would have done so.

Currie's public persona caused him to be loved and loathed. He revelled in acclaim, whether it came from an individual or from hundreds in a concert hall. In truth, he needed it desperately. Not only as the adrenalin which inspires public figures and performers, but also as reassurance that he was not a flop, not 'the abject failure' who left West Pilton with his life in tatters. All his life he trod that

19

tightrope. He needed praise and admiration. But even one critic in that hall of hundreds would depress him and overrule the praise. It almost seems that he wanted to fail.

'James needed to be bolstered and supported,' Peggy said. 'He took everything so personally. It was as if sometimes he thought the whole world was against him. When he was in a black mood he was hell to live with. Not just for me. The boys got it too, all the folk who meant most to him.

'But that's just the way he was. Folk wouldn't believe it. I often felt that he wallowed in his despair, but you can't just tell someone to "snap out of it". Depression's not like that. You simply had to wait till the right time and offer plenty of encouragement and love.'

What were James's best qualities? 'Affection. He was very affectionate, a most affectionate man.'

That's the man the people of Pollok knew and loved. What they didn't know was that they got most of his affection. Often when he got home he had none left for his family. His sons, 'just seemed to grow up around me. That's my one big regret. I missed my boys growing up. I never seemed to have the time to give them.'

James Currie kept a diary throughout the years of his ministry. The entries are those of a businessman, appointments, bills to pay, and a record of his innermost thoughts. His love, pride and hopes for his sons are set out almost daily. After his death, James, his eldest, Charles and Iain read the diaries. To a man they said: 'I never knew father felt that way. I wish I had known.'

Currie was many things. But first and foremost he was a servant of God.

CHAPTER THREE

'You're not going to give up now'

Coincidence, fate, divine intervention – each explanation is equally valid because as James Currie got off the ferry at Brodick after leaving West Pilton and the ministry 'forever' in 1947 it started to snow and forgot to stop. The warmer waters of the North Atlantic Drift keep summers cooler and winters milder and usually restrict snowfalls on the island to a thin blanket, but that month saw Arran's worst blizzard in living memory.

James had never quarrelled seriously with his parents. He was brought up in the auld Scots tradition that they knew best and he must obey. He had not had reason to question their judgment and had been a dutiful son. But when he arrived unannounced at Drumadoon that day he was curt to the point of rudeness.

'Don't ask. Just don't ask me.'

Any parents will know how they longed to comfort and guide their son. The fact that they respected his need for solitude is testament of the obvious enormity of his anguish. Peggy was at college in Glasgow studying agriculture. James was glad. He wanted to be left alone.

The snow continued to fall. As it rose over the dry stane dykes of the island James felt as if it was enveloping him in a white cocoon. He had no plans – only one solid commitment – never to return to his job in West Pilton.

As he relived his feelings he wept openly and unashamedly. The predominant emotion was one of relief, a release from the onerous responsibilities which almost broke him. But all too soon that comforting indulgence was to be swept away by the despair of admitting that was 'an abject failure'.

The thriving Bible Class, Sunday School and youth clubs he had left behind were not compensation. He had given his best and knew it had not been good enough. At the age of twenty-six, his life was in shreds; his spirit broken; his mind in turmoil. But he was strong of body and eager for the manual labour which would devour the daylight and

Young and confident and working on Iona.

bring rest from physical exhaustion at night. Each morning he was relieved to wake up in his own bed. But the shroud of reality would rapidly envelop him and he had to live with himself for another day.

When the snow stopped falling fierce winds whipped up drifts which buried farm houses and cottages on the island. After clearing a path from Drumadoon into the village of Blackwaterfoot, James joined a

22

team of volunteers to help to dig out families literally buried in their homes. In emergencies, where the drifts were more than forty feet deep, the rescuers wrapped bread, bottles of milk, and bacon in bags and lowered them down chimneys.

The folk of Arran form a close-knit community, and in the midst of his personal problems the cameraderie helped to ease James's mind. The telephone lines had been blown down, all ship crossings from the mainland had been cancelled, so his beloved island was in splendid isolation. All his worries were across the water and, as he stood on a frozen drift and hung his jacket on the top of a telephone pole and set to work with a shovel, he laughed aloud. His hands and face, the only parts exposed to the biting wind, were stinging with the 'burn' from the freezing conditions. His eyes were screwed to slits in an attempt to diminish the blinding whiteness of the sun's glare off the snow. The laughter was invigorating. Now he could accept that his vocation was a fallacy. It had brought him scurrying home, beaten and broken, because there was nothing else he could think of doing, nowhere else he could go. But he could dig and sow and reap. He believed then he would never be fit for the ardour of the pulpit, but he could yoke himself to the plough. Was that not what he had always wanted to do? As his health returned, so too did the yearning for the Church.

The plough or the pulpit? The dichotomy was to haunt him.

The interlude provided by the blizzard was brief. When Arran rejoined the outside world the repercussions of James's 'defection' struck swiftly. Elders from West Pilton telephoned in dismay at being 'let down'. Allan Easton was 'hurt'. George MacLeod sent what should have been the perfect conciliatory letter: 'Meet you at dawn – pistols for two: coffee for one.'

But no one realised how near the young man was to breaking point. He could be neither coaxed nor bullied back to the cloth. Even when his dear Mrs Fraser offered to send on the treasured possessions he had left in her home James told her to set fire to them. Burning his bridges lest he be tempted to go back . . .

The work of a minister and a farmer may be diverse, but the hours are similar. The day is never long enough to complete the workload. So it was on Drumadoon. The farm is situated at the south-west of Arran, near Blackwaterfoot. Its 650 acres are hilly, covered in heather and bracken. Over the years careful cultivation has brought the reward of a few acres of better grazing capable of supporting a few dairy cattle, but the majority of the land is suitable only for hardy sheep. Long, arduous hours of ploughing with Clydesdales was Currie's 'treatment'.

Drumadoon was an important part of his life. It was his birthplace, his refuge, his pride and joy – and in latter years a millstone around his neck. The farm and the Currie family have been linked for more than one hundred years, and the partnership has brought a great deal of controversy.

Around 1850, the population of the island was about 6000 and falling steadily. At that time Peter Currie was tenant of Glenloig, forty acres of moorland on the perimeter of Drumadoon. He had a handful of sheep and one dairy cow. How he managed to provide for six children is a feat which can only be admired. The croft was rented from the Duke of Hamilton, whose descendants own large estates on Arran to this day. The tenancy of Glenloig would go to Peter's first-born son, who was named after him. As the second son, James knew from an early age he would have to make his own way in life and this, and a thirst for adventure, stretched his horizons far beyond Arran.

Britannia ruled the waves and Britain's empire was thriving. Before his twentieth birthday, young James set sail on a trading ship for the West Indies. His destination, Tobago, gave him the nickname which is still used today when Arran folk talk about him. And there is still plenty to talk about.

Tobago got work on a sugar plantation, and although the climate was a complete contrast to that of his native island, his expertise was soon evident. Any man who can work the stony soil of Arran in the teeth of an Atlantic wind has little to learn about hard labour. Remarkably, the young man was put in charge of the plantation.

As in all families, the successes are documented in full but the disappointments are recorded in monosyllables. For some unexplained reason Tobago Currie returned to Arran. Perhaps homesickness, the sorceress, had woven her spell of delusion. Whatever the reason, soon after returning he realised that Arran's grass was still a pale green and once more set sail for the West Indies. he got his job back and prospered, attaining a position and wealth he could only have dreamed about on Glenloig. When he married the daughter of the Governor of Tobago his future seemed as bright as the Caribbean sun. But again, unhappiness possessed him. His wife died and he came back to Arran, not knowing what he was looking for but hoping to find it in the hills of his childhood. He did not, and the spring of 1878 saw him sitting on Brodick pier waiting once more for the ferry to take him to the mainland on the first leg of another voyage back to the West Indies.

In farming attire with sister Jean and Peggy.

What were his thoughts? He had left Tobago under a cloud and now his dejection was affecting his family on Arran. He had chased his destiny but found only disillusionment. These interpretations may be pure supposition, but they are given credence by Tobago's grandson who sat on the same pier seventy years later experiencing those same emotions. James Currie knew that Tobago understood what it was to be an 'abject failure'.

Tobago had a benefactor in the shape of the then Duke of Hamilton. He had heard the young man speak at a Tory meeting and had been impressed. He saw the potential in the disillusioned explorer, plagued by wanderlust and homesickness. It took few words to persuade Tobago to stay.

The duke told him, 'Arran can ill afford to lose young men like you. Go home and I will consider you for the next farm which becomes vacant.'

It is interesting to note that Tobago's Conservative leanings, if they existed at all, were short-lived. It is much more likely that he had begun a campaign to impress the duke. His politics, which have been passed on to the Currie clan, were staunchly socialist.

If Tobago was considered for the next vacant tenancies then he was found wanting. It was two years before the duke was convinced that he had acquired the responsibility to merit a chance. And the tenancy he was given caused a great deal of acrimony on the island. Drumadoon may be far from the ideal farm, but it was considered one of the better tenancies on Arran. When it fell vacant, some of the more mature men who had tilled a living on small, infertile crofts staked their claim to it. The duke's decision to give it to Tobago was controversial and unpopular. But the deal had its price.

The rent was set at £280 a year – a figure which remained constant for the following fifty years until it was reassessed at £89! Tobago at last settled down and married a local girl. Soon Janey was born and then James.

Years later Arran was again to be divided over the decision to grant tenancy of the farm to a Currie, this time when the Revd James Currie was selected after the death of his father. But the row did not end there. After much legal wrangling the minister succeeded in buying Drumadoon. It was the realisation of an ambition, and the beginning of a financial millstone. In 1962 the farm was more than £4500 in the red. Months after James's death Peggy was forced to sell part of the land to pay off debts. Her accountant suggested ways of winning time, but she knew it was a losing battle. Though it almost broke her heart she told him to sell.

'When do I stop selling?' he asked.

'When the debts are cleared,' she replied.

'Even if that means selling Drumadoon?' he cautioned.

'Even if that means selling Drumadoon.'

It didn't . . . for the meantime.

If the ministry was temporarily to lose the labours of James Currie, the farm was gaining them. Tobago had started the back-breaking task of cultivating the soil. It was thin and sandy, covered in heather and whin bushes with stubborn, interwoven roots. There seemed to be more stone than soil and boulders which could take hours to dig out. Once the ground was tilled, the sea winds would whip off topsoil, exposing more roots and stones. But the winds which brought so many problems also yielded a bonus.

As it tormented the sea, each tide threw up 'reck', seaweed rich in nitrogen. This was the ideal agent for binding and nourishing the soil. Tobago began wresting bush and boulder from the land and depositing them on the beach, and hauling the seaweed the few hundred yards up the steep hill of the Doon. The job was eternal: progress agonisingly slow and arduous, but his resolve did not weaken. As the challenge was handed down from father to son, so too did the offspring of the faithful Clydesdales take over the yoke.

The tradition became an obsession: a contest with Mother Nature; the prize of each acre another chapter in the family's history. In the autumn of 1947 the young clergyman thought he had written the final paragraphs and the conclusion was a miserable defeat.

He had laboured for days at a few square yards where the whins were thickest and the boulders huge. He was up to his waist digging at one rock and had yet to ascertain its size. James had fastened ropes around it and his horse struggled to shift it as he attempted to lever it free with a sturdy stave. It was no good.

'I'm wasting my time,' he said.

The sweat lost here could be used more productively. As the surveyed the yards he had gained he knew he had done as well as any man. There is a time to end every battle: the moment to call a halt and begin something fresh.

James had reached that time. But his father had not.

James had left the pulpit weeks before. His reasons had not been discussed, nor were they to be. But his father recognised that this was a moment which would make or break his son.

27

He said simply: 'James, you're not going to give up now.'

He did not raise his voice, did not wait for a protest or any reaction at all.

James Currie fought that boulder until darkness fell. Even then he did not stop. No one saw it being removed from the ground. When he returned to the farmhouse everyone had gone to bed. The victory was his alone.

That small corner of Drumadoon is far from its most productive land, but it is the most treasured. The stones which came out of the soil were stored around the edge of the field. Years later James used them to build a dry stane dyke. It was a labour of love. He believed that there was a place for every stone, and never cut one.

The novelist would have used this triumph in the field as a turning point to relaunch his hero's career, a stepping stone to destiny. But although James Currie's health was returning he was as far from the ministry as he ever would be. The only pulpit he could see was in West Pilton and that was in the past. He was yoked to the plough . . . and happy with it.

CHAPTER FOUR

The playground minister

James Currie was born at Drumadoon on 16 January 1921, the first of James and Jessie Anne Currie's six children. He took great pride in his humble background and his childhood memories were remarkably clear.

Farming is not simply an occupation – and an extremely demanding one – it is more a way of life which can be accepted by few who are not born to it. Children are reared in an industrious environment and, from an early age, are allocated their chores. Young James was aware of his responsibility of being heir to the tenancy of Drumadoon long before he went to school. Tobago's inheritance was not to be abused.

James's father was the dominant parent: six foot two inches tall with a strong, muscular frame hardened in the fields, and a strict, Calvinistic attitude to match. He was highly respected on Arran, and received the island's ultimate accolade of being referred to by name of his farm. Like many powerful men he had a great respect for his strength, regarding it as a gift not to be abused or displayed. James could remember only one occasion when frustration overruled his father's modesty.

A relative's car, a solid Ford, was halted by a puncture and the delay in jacking it up annoyed the tenant of Drumadoon. In anger, he lifted the rear of the vehicle three feet off the ground and held it there while a sufficient number of stones were gathered to place under the axle. He quickly regretted his bravado and forbade his proud son from speaking about it.

Young James idolised his father and tried to live in his image. This impossible task for a boy was compounded by Drumadoon's demands that he should be perfect in word and deed. James Currie senior was the archetypal Scotsman: the provider who rarely shows his feelings, especially to his son and heir who will have to take over the burden of responsibility.

Among Drumadoon's greatest assets were his modesty and selflessness. These qualities meant much to him and he was determined that his son should attain them. To do this, he ruled the boy with a rod of

Young James with Jenny *and* Elsa.

iron. Young James was the only one to see this side of the strict disciplinarian and was envious of the affection his father displayed to other members of the family and casual acquaintances. The boy craved his father's open affection, but the chemistry could not be changed and it exaggerated the boy's lack of confidence. In his eyes his father could do no wrong. If he could not please Drumadoon, he must be a failure.

The farmer must have thought he was doing his best to prepare his son for the rigours of later life. Providence had forced him and his own father to leave Scotland in their youth. If James Currie the third had to face such an ordeal he should have the character to meet it, and Drumadoon was determined that he would. The boy finally accepted his father's approach, but could not reconcile the fact that when he needed affection he felt cut off.

'Don't make too much of that,' he said. 'Father was a kind, deeply compassionate man. He loved me and I always knew that. It's just that I never seemed able to please him.'

In later life, when his son had fulfilled his demands, Drumadoon found nothing too much trouble to please his son. He was proud of James's achievements, and displayed this pride openly.

30

But the traumatic childhood left its scars in later life. When James was called upon to enter a new sphere the trepidation which was so evident in his childhood was rekindled. Experience and confidence were extinguished by the threat of the unknown, achievements were forgotten, and the smouldering fear of 'being found out' returned. Familiar fields disguised no dangers: breaking new ground might expose one's own shallowness. And James Currie was in no doubt that he was a man of very limited talent.

'I'm so ordinary,' he said. 'And people expect someone special.' His professionalism and ability to perform usually ensured that was what they got.

James was six years old when he first went to Shiskine primary. His shyness and lack of confidence were acute. He often burst into tears when he had to speak to someone outwith his immediate family. He was a big lad, towering conspicuously over the remainder of the school's first year intake – a grand total of three. His introduction to school had been delayed because of his untimely 'death'.

He had been born with a hernia and, although it caused no suffering, it necessitated an operation. When the boy was four, Dr Balfour, a frequent guest at Drumadoon, decided the time was right for the boy to go into Lamlash Hospital. Everything went according to plan until the anaesthetic was administered and the young heart stopped beating. Some fifty years later he would be taken to that same hospital after suffering a heart attack.

Sixty years ago medical equipment was much less sophisticated and the island hospital was stocked only with the necessities. The expertise of the medical team revived the small heart but it was considered to be too dangerous to go ahead with the operation. James was detained for a few days, but no indications could be found as to why he had reacted so dramatically to the anaesthetic. It was decided that he should spend some time under the watchful eyes of his parents.

James' family was not noted for scholastic excellence and, ironically, his shyness and lack of confidence were the major factors which forged his path of academic distinction. From the beginning he compensated for what he lacked in inspiration with plenty of perspiration, which enabled him to complete primary one in three months and join up with children of his own age. Later that determination would see him to the top of university classes.

If a six year old can be a swot then James Currie was one. But he would willingly have exchanged his classroom achievements for a portion of the confidence of some of the more precocious boys.

Nicknames which endure a lifetime are bestowed at this age, and the number of 'Wee Ecks' who grew to six feet prove the transience of their validity. However the accuracy of the youngsters' assessment of James is a testament to how astute children can be. After a few days at school he was referred to by one and all as 'The Minister'. Out of the mouths of babes and sucklings . . .

Master Currie's lack of confidence might have prevented him from taking a leading role in school proceedings, but it enabled him to stand back and observe. Shiskine playground was the foundation of his talent as a shrewd assessor of character. His endeavours to be a member of John MacDougall's team, no matter the game, is an early example. The young MacDougall was not the most gifted of participants, but he was unparalleled in the field of vociferous and tenacious argument. His side was often outplayed but never outman-oeuvred. MacDougall never lost a playground conflict and James learned the lesson of utilising the talents of others at an early age.

Around this time the ability to stand back and examine the development of another incident made a lasting impression on 'The Minister'. The pupils were not allowed to enter the schoolhouse until the bell rang at nine o'clock. Some children had defied this rule and in the course of their boisterous play the headmaster's daughter, Seonaid Smith, had her fingers badly crushed in the school door. The injuries were severe and, in his anxiety and anger, the headmaster threatened to belt every pupil. In the event, he did not carry out the punishment for innocent and guilty alike, but the incident offended young James's sense of justice and turned him against violence of any description. These childhood memories had a remarkably strong influence on his views on life.

Drumadoon farm attracted a succession of labourers who never failed to interest James. Tom Smith, a pest control expert, was the least popular, a dour man who hogged the fire and cursed when the children tried to warm themselves.

Martin Callow would arrive at the farm unexpectedly and disappear just as swiftly. He was about five foot eight inches tall, slim, with sandy coloured hair and sharp, pointed features. He was a man with a mysterious past. His cultured voice and extensive knowledge of literature indicated an expensive education, but he offered no explanation of how he came to be living a rough life, and none was sought. He seemed to accept his incongruous role as part of life's flotsam without complaint, and willingly performed the vital, but dirty task, of keeping the burns, which flowed past the fields, free of blockages.

At lunch time, James's mother would hang a white cloth on the farm gate to show that the meal was ready. On one occasion Martin Callow was busy working in a hollow and did not see the cloth. When James was sent to fetch him the man looked surprised. He said: 'I did not hear you. I was listening to the babbling of the brook as it went on its way.' Inevitably, he too went on his way and the children waited in vain for his return. They liked to think that he did not come back because he had settled in a way of life more suited to his talents.

Geordie 'Swallow' Long arrived with the birds on the first day of each spring. A big, strong Irishman, he would work long and hard until the leaves began to change colour then, as the swallows gathered in preparation for their winter migration, Swallow would walk into Brodick, drink his fill, and come back to pick a fight with Drumadoon Currie. The pattern never changed. It was almost as if he could not say goodbye, and preferred to leave under a cloud. But the following spring, the altercation forgiven and forgotten, Swallow would reappear.

Drumadoon welcomed men who could turn their hand to anything in return for bed and board and a few pounds in their pocket when they chose to leave. James's mother described Iain Macdonald as one such bird of passage, 'here today, gone tomorrow'. But the man settled into the family and stayed for many years. When the children discovered he was uncomfortable in the company of women, they teased him and invented romances with local girls. His reply was always the same: 'No' her – she's got a face like last year's rhubarb.' When James left primary school for Keil College in Dumbarton, 'Rhubarb Roots' gave him a watch. His kindness and generosity was fully appreciated, but later the man was to make a more valuable contribution to James Currie's life.

One of young James's chores before school in the morning was to take maize from the barn to the sheep. On more than one occasion he would be greeted with two feet sticking out from beneath old sacks – the signal that Martin Webster had returned during the night. Martin was an orphan who had been brought up in Quarrier's Homes and earned a living at farms throughout south-west Scotland. Though James liked the youth, and got on well with him, secretly he dreaded seeing Martin again because it meant he would lose the tenuous link he had with his father.

The orphan had a willing surrogate father in Drumadoon Currie, and the farmer found that he could confide in the youth. The unlikely friendship was known all over the island, and stood the test of time.

One day, while the two were at a stack forking corn for threshing, Drumadoon asked Martin what he would choose if granted one wish. The youth, who had no home and precious few possessions, thought carefully before replying: 'If the Lord would allow it, I would like to live for ever.'

The sight of the pair tramping the hills, so happy in each other's company, induced feelings of guilt and envy in young James. He could not get close to his father but this unlikely youth, just a few years senior to him, had won the farmer's trust and affection. Years later Martin came back to the farm with a fine young woman by his side. If the Lord had granted his wish he could not have been happier. 'Mr Currie,' he announced proudly, 'meet my wife.'

James treasured the time spent with his father, most of it working and being trained in the many skills required to run a farm. During a lesson in how to put up a fence, the boy was holding nails while his father hammered them into a post. It is to be expected that in the course of a day's work Drumadoon's concentration would lapse. He struck the boy's fingers a painful blow – and did not say a word or express any indication of emotion. His fingers sore and bleeding, James was not allowed to cry, but had to carry on as if nothing had happened. It is difficult to imagine the man's feelings, but his determination that his son would be prepared for life's blows is evident.

James was a timid boy. 'A big softie, a coward, really,' he said. 'I suppose my father saw that and didn't like it. He must have been trying to make me into a man, but he cowed me, browbeat me. I was afraid of father, but I can't remember him lifting his hand to me in anger.'

If the farmer's tactics to toughen his son appear excessively harsh, an attempt should be made to examine how he could have felt at the time. There can be little doubt that he was disappointed in the boy, and was embarrassed by his son's emotional outbursts. On one occasion, when sent to deliver a simple message to his aunt, James got into a panic and wept uncontrollably for ten minutes.

Drumadoon was a practical man, and decided his son would have to confront his problems to overcome them. During a visit to a ceilidh in Pinmill school, James was aghast when Drumadoon ordered him on to the stage to sing. His rendition of *Bonnie Strathyre* left a lot to be desired, but in finishing the song he recorded a major victory.

The farmer chose another testing ground with great care. Legend has it that Robert the Bruce learned to try, try, try again from a spider in the King's Caves, on land now belonging to Drumadoon. The caves were also used as a place of worship when Christians were persecuted, and many a grisly tale is told of bloody encounters in the area. When James was six, his father took him to cave known as Ogham and offered him one penny to follow the route said to have been taken by a piper who went in the entrance, marched through the hills, and emerged miles away. The boy was terrified, but he squeezed into the tight, dank passage, overcoming his fear and earning his penny.

Another childhood memory is of Annie Currie, who ran a boarding house called Greannan, a mile over the hill from Drumadoon. She maintained that the best time to visit Glasgow was during its fair fortnight 'when the locals were away on holiday', and this she did once a year leaving a brief note of explanation for her paying guests and an open invitation to 'feel free to help yourselves to food from the larder.' Annie's youngest sister, Mary, was wooed by a suitor who did not meet with Annie's approval. Her acerbic remarks were ignored by the young Lochinvar, so Annie decided the situation required more drastic action.

One evening, as the young couple settled cosily before a roaring fire in the front room, Annie cut a divot from the lawn, climbed on to the roof, and planted the divot firmly over the chimney. The couple emerged from the house spluttering to find Annie sitting defiantly on the divot on the chimney! The heat went out of the young man's passion after that. Neither sister married and they ran the boarding house successfully until tragedy struck. One morning when Mary was starting the electricity generator her clothing became entangled in the machinery and she could not get free. Annie heard the cries for help and ran to her sister's aid. Mary was crushed to death and Annie's leg was broken in her struggles to help. This was one of young James's first encounters with death.

On New Year's Eve, 1932, James was sent to Balnacoole to invite friends to a party at Drumadoon. There was a strong wind at his back and he quickly covered the four miles on his new racing bicycle. A tall hawthorn hedge broke the blast from the wind as he prepared to cross the bridge over the Clachan burn. He was travelling at a good speed when he left the shelter of the hedge and moved on to the bridge. Suddenly a fierce gust lifted the bicycle and the boy was thrown over the parapet. He fell about twelve feet, landing head first on a jagged rock. James's recollections of the next few minutes are confused, but he reckoned he was knocked out and brought back to consciousness by the icy water.

35

Johnny Nicol, the postman, appeared with his pony and trap and when the animal saw the blood gushing from the boy's skull it reared up and bolted. Johnny helped James from the water and Mrs Murchie, who had seen the accident from her farmhouse window, hurried down to take him into the warmth of her kitchen. Blood is stinging his eyes; it is spattered on the woman's wrap-around pinnie, and soaking a large towel. Dr Rutherford appears, there is the smell of ether, and Uncle John drives James home in his car.

The arrival at Drumadoon was crystal-clear in James's mind. His father, who had been playing golf on the course which runs close to the farm, had been informed and was pacing the road. The car had barely stopped when he pulled open the door and cradled the boy in his arms. Father's tears mixed with his son's blood. A number of stitches had been inserted in the head wound and the boy's top teeth had been broken, but the strained relationship between father and son had been healed and James thought: 'It was worth it. It really was.'

The injury kept James off school for the month of January. To recuperate, he was taken to Parkhouse, his Aunt Janey's farm. On 25 January she arranged a Burns Supper. The only other guest was a lodger, who had been a doctor in Trinidad. Like so many members of his profession the doctor had started to take strong drink, then the drink took a drink, and finally the drink was taking the man. He had left Trinidad for Arran, where he received a modest monthly allowance from some benefactor. It was sufficient to live on, but small enough to limit his consumption of alcohol. It was in this unusual company that James Currie first addressed the haggis:

Fair fa' yir honest sonsie face

Great chieftain o' the pudden race . . .

The boy who used to tremble and weep when he had to speak to his aunt had matured. In later life his unique style, ready wit, and appraisal of Burns would be appreciated by tens of thousands. But perhaps that early memory had another impact. James Currie hated drink. Or, more accurately, he hated the abuse of alcohol. He did not drink himself, and was strongly opposed to those who saw Burns nights as an excuse for a booze-up.

The boy was growing big, broad and strong. A fine son to take over and continue the progress of the Curries at Drumadoon. His father must have been reassured to see the boy work willingly and take a genuine interest in the farm, but his development in another sphere was equally pleasing. Drumadoon Currie was a deeply religious man.

On Sundays up to seventy folk gathered at Drumadoon for hymn-singing. On fine nights they would worship outdoors, lifting their eyes and voices to the hills. Other evenings would be spent round the harmonium in the farmhouse. Ever eager to emulate his father, James had acquired a love of the scriptures.

In the winter of 1933 a new pupil arrived at Shiskine primary. John McPhee was taciturn and moody, which was ample excuse for most of the children to avoid him. They were, after all, from a close-knit community and any stranger was treated with suspicion. Furthermore, this boy was not the cleanest of individuals. His clothes were ill-fitting and reeked of wood smoke; his hair was badly cut; and his complexion could charitably have been described as weather-beaten, which indeed it was, but it also suffered because of its infrequent encounters with soap and water. John McPhee was a tinker's son. His family was forced to spend the winter in the other set of caves – the Queen's Caves, the sanctuary where the persecuted Christians had worshipped. This was to be the tinker's boy's home during the worst weather of the year. The lad was not bright, a handicap compounded by his lack of schooling as his father led the family on a peripatetic path in an attempt to earn a crust.

James befriended the boy and invited his family to Drumadoon for dinner. As he broke this news to his parents, he realised it would have been wiser to have first asked their permission before extending hospitality, but his kindness was greeted with pleasure. It would not be the first time members of the travelling fraternity had been made welcome at the farm. A man's man for a' that . . . James could remember the look of surprise on the face of Jock Townsley, who had called at the door peddling his wares and had been invited in for a meal. The man's discomfiture disappeared in the friendly atmosphere and he made himself at home. As he stood in front of the fire, raising the back of his shabby, herringbone jacket to heat his houghs, he must have felt completely at ease. So much so, that he cleared his throat noisily and was about to project the unsavoury mouthful on to the fireside rug when he remembered he was in a family livingroom. However, he was beyond the point of no return so, with as much dignity as he could muster, he used his inside jacket pocket as a spittoon! The McPhee family became frequent visitors to Drumadoon, but their visits were never quite so spectacular as that of Mr Townsley.

James attended Sunday School in Shiskine from the age of six. He was enthralled by the stories from the Bible, and his vivid imagination brought them to life in settings around the island of Arran. The Red Sea parted in Blackwaterfoot bay. Moses received the tablets at the Doon. Christ was crucified on the hill above Drumadoon. He had a suitable location for each story he learned, and, as he walked past these spots the Bible took on a fresh and living significance.

The minister of the parish at that time was one of the old school, who served up fire and brimstone with much weeping, wailing and gnashing of teeth. The threat of eternal damnation was never far away. As the young boy sat through a particularly sombre sermon, his attention was caught by a beautiful tortoiseshell butterfly in a panic at a stained-glass window, desperate to get out of the church and into the sunlight. The scene returned to him often, and he vowed that his Church would not be one of threats. Currie's kirk preached the Word, and it often rang with laughter.

In June, 1932, James went to Lochranza to sit a bursary examination for Keil College. His father could not afford to pay the college fees, and was delighted when it was learned that his son had passed the examination and would receive a bursary. James was with his Aunt Janey at Parkhouse when his father brought the news. To celebrate, the boy was allowed to play his favourite record on Aunt Janey's gramophone. He did not know the words would be prophetic, and that after a period of calm he would once more be cast adrift in turbulent waters. The words from the well-worn record hovered in the still evening air . . . 'Softly and tenderly Jesus is calling.'

Keil held many terrors for young James, but it was the making of him. Not once, but twice. Its headmaster, James Mason, saw the potential in the raw farmer's son, and became the most powerful influence in his life.

CHAPTER FIVE

Master mason

Shortly after arriving at Keil, James wrote to his parents: 'It's really nice . . . I just wish you were here.' Of course, in the strange surroundings, he had retreated into his shell of shyness. But Keil held two aces which would bring the boy on by leaps and bounds – James Mason and rugby.

Drumadoon Currie had tried as best he knew how to make a man of his son. James Mason saw the boy's finer qualities and nurtured them. This process took five years and meant that James Currie was not being educated to return to the fields of Arran, but to go out into the ministry. As in his first days at primary school, 'The Minister's' destiny seemed preordained. But he had to acquire some confidence, (or was it self-esteem?), before that could take place. The rugby field gave him much of what was required.

As a boy, he was a Rangers fanatic. There was no wireless at Drumadoon, so he used to run to the house of Hugh Mathieson, the greenkeeper of the golf course, to find out how his team had fared each Saturday. He had always hoped to go to Keil College, which concentrated on 'practical things like agricultural studies and technical subjects,' but one thing peeved him. The uniform. It was green. Green blazer with yellow badge and piping, and green and yellow socks. For a Rangers supporter that was hard to bear. Football was banned at Keil where every boy, unless he had a medical certificate to the contrary, was obliged to play rugby. Currie took to it like a duck to water.

He was a big, strong lad and, after he had been whacked a few times on the field, relished the physical challenge. As his expertise grew, so too did his stature among his fellows. He was respected on and off the field.

His early memories of Keil days were unhappy ones. When a teacher called him by his surname, common practice in the public school system, Currie cried. By way of explanation, he said that he had dreamt his grandmother had died and it had upset him. After class, he confided in a chum who thought the real reason amusing and told other boys. When he discovered that his secret was out, Currie was angry and embarrassed. But he had learned another childhood lesson that was to be a watchword for the rest of his life.

'I'm careful not to tell anyone about my own private business,' he said. 'You've got to keep your distance. It is true that familiarity breeds contempt.'

James Mason was a great believer in the system of boy-government. The pupils were responsible for much of the day-to-day running of the school, including making their beds and keeping dormitories clean and tidy, and maintenance of the thirty-two acres of gardens. The boys were split into squads of ten, each with its chief, who supervised chores and administered discipline. Currie hated, 'and to this day I find it difficult not to hate', the boy in charge of the first squad to which he was attached. 'He was cruel and unjust. A bully.'

On two occasions after the lights had gone out and the boys should have been sleeping, the squad chief heard boys talking. James, and other boys who had been sleeping, were roused from sleep by their chief to be given the strap. The incident appalled him and when he was made senior chief, in charge of all the boys at the college, he approached James Mason and asked if corporal punishment could be abolished. The headmaster readily agreed. By way of punishment boys were obliged to work in the gardens or clean lavatories. The system 'worked just great'.

James was twelve when he went to the college. Some of the boys in his class were fourteen or fifteen, and he found the studies demanding. He worked hard, and came first in almost every exam. He said he felt 'cheated out of the *dux* medal', claiming that Mr Mason had put forward a boy for a scholarship and 'must have felt obliged to make him *dux*.' Nevertheless, to come second in a school noted for its excellence was a feat which had not been expected – not even by the demanding Drumadoon.

James Currie spoke with passion about his days on the rugby field. He was a fine player, a wing-forward, who played for Glasgow against Edinburgh and later for Boroughmuir. The Keil team, of which he became captain, was all-conquering. Currie, its place-kicker, practised for hours on end. As he related the events of a game against Allan Glen's, whose team was unbeaten, his eyes lit up.

'We were losing with a few minutes to go when I got the ball on my own twenty-five yard line. I set off, dribbled through their entire team, passed then got the ball back and scored a try. Then I converted the kick. We won eight-six. What a game! What a day! It was glorious, just glorious!

James in rugby days wearing Keil College strip.

James Mason, who was watching the game, must have had a glow of satisfaction. He had taken a particular interest in the ungainly young boy, seeing beyond his shyness and lack of confidence. When James was thirteen, he walked into the rose garden at the college with his headmaster. He did not remember what was discussed, 'but it wasn't religion', or how long the conversation lasted.

'I walked into the rose garden wanting to be a farmer. And when I walked out I told Mr Mason I wanted to be a minister. It was as simple as that.'

The playground phrophesy was being fulfilled. Simple at the time, but much soul-searching and anguish was to follow.

James Mason, a deeply religious man, liked to have 'a minister from every year.' To the best of James's knowledge, his mentor had never discussed the question of a career with Drumadoon, who also had a hankering for his son to become a man of God. James himself had never considered that he might pursue any other work than farming. As an only son, he knew it was his duty to take over Drumadoon, and was only too happy to do so. Surely he must have realised, as he 'saw' Moses on the Doon or the Red Sea parting in Blackwaterfoot bay, that the pulpit was beckoning?

'I never thought about it for a minute,' he said. 'The farm was the only job I considered. I don't know what came over me in the rose garden. I don't know what we were talking about. I don't know why I said that I wanted to be a minister, but that was it. Although I had doubts later, I told my father of my decision and he was happy about it. Honestly, like everything else in my life, it all happened by accident.'

Keil took boys from all sections of society. Some, like James, were from humble homes and 'suffered the hardship of washing our own clothes.' Others were from wealthy families – 'some of them real pukka sahib.' One day the boys were out walking when they passed workmen digging a ditch by the side of the road.

'Is that you James?' said a voice from the ditch.

It was Rhubarb Roots, the labourer from Drumadoon who had given the boy his wristwatch. James was delighted to see his old friend. The man did not appear to have changed, his lined face still smeared with the honest toil of the earth. When the boy stopped to speak to an ordinary roaddigger, he was teased and chided by some of his fellow pupils. To his great regret, James spent but little time with the workman, but he never forgot the incident or the lesson he learned from it . . . a man's a man for a' that.

He left Keil with great regret and went on to the arts faculty of Glasgow University. He wrote later that his three years there were 'the unhappiest of my life'. James Mason had made him promise that would not join any organisations at the university, saying: 'You will have plenty to do coping with your studies.' And Currie studied hard. He was adamant that he was not, clever. 'I was a slave to note-taking. Each morning I took down as much as I could of the lecture, then rewrote it at home in the afternoon. Every night I swotted up what I had written.' He dismissed the whole university process as a waste of time. 'In the same way preaching is pointless unless the man in the pulpit makes a living contact with the man in the pew.'

While he was at university war broke out. There was never any question in his mind over whether he would go to fight. He was a committed pacifist. Now was the time to stand up for what he believed in. James, who was living with his Aunt May in Dennistoun, had to go to Parkhead Labour Exchange to register as a conscientious objector. The official who dealt with him 'more or less accused me of being a coward. I can remember the hatred in his eyes and the vitriol on his lips as he said: "You're just scared they will cancel your reservation and you'll have to go and fight." I was too shy to argue.'

Currie was not a coward, and he knew that sometimes it takes more courage not to fight.

No matter the weather, James wore his overcoat while attending lectures. This, naturally, attracted attention, the very thing he was trying to avoid. But he was hiding a dark secret. His Aunt May had given him a pair of trousers which he felt were too short and tight at the knees. He thought he looked ridiculous, but could not bring himself to tell his aunt. So he wore the toursers – and his overcoat. Once a week, he had a lecture in the afternoon. His aunt gave him sandwiches. While his fellow students mingled over lunch in common rooms or on park benches, Currie ate his sandwiches locked in a lavatory.

'Some people will ridicule me for my stupidity as they read this, but I am being strictly honest for the sake of others who suffer the agony of feeling different or detached. The great majority of people have no difficulty in attaching themselves to the herd, but others, like me, are terrified of being rebuffed or hurt.'

Currie once more excelled in his studies, and graduated Master of Arts in June 1941. He made little or no impact on the university, and left it gladly.

The following three years at Trinity College, studying for his

Bachelor of Divinity, were happy and full of fellowship. The brotherhood of spirit bolstered him so much that he forgot his shyness. Even meal times were happy occasions! He was amazed to find himself talking and laughing with students who shared lectures at Glasgow University. Such 'ogres' as James Martin, James Aitchison, James Paterson, James Shirra and John MacKelvie went on to become Church of Scotland ministers and lifelong friends.

Again Currie achieved academic distinction, and his Bachelor of Divinity, which set him on course for West Pilton.

He could not speak about his days in that parish without reliving the anguish which almost broke him. In our tape-recorded conversations when the subject arose his voice dropped to little more than a whisper as he relived the painful memories. More than once, he burst into tears. This was the man James Mason went to see at Drumadoon, the man who had turned his back on the Kirk, the man who wanted only to be with his family on his family's farm.

James had married Peggy in April 1947, months after returning from Edinburgh. Just over a year later, their first son, called James naturally, was born. There was no doubt in the proud young father's mind where his future lay: it was in the soil of his father and grandfather. He had rejected outright all appeals to return to West Pilton and the ministry. He had attempted to serve the pulpit and it had almost broken him, now he was content with the plough. There was only one man who could override this contentment and in the summer of 1948 he arrived unannounced at Drumadoon.

James Mason had a vacancy for and English master at Keil. Currie was the man for the job, Mason would not take 'No' for an answer. He bolstered the failed minister, boosted his ego, and he offered a salary. James would stay at the college, and this would enable him to save more in one year than he could in ten at Drumadoon. Money had never been important to him, but now he had a wife and son. He complied with James Mason's wishes and took up residence in Keil for the first term of 1948.

It was an excellent career move. He got on well with both the boys and his fellow teachers. The acid test came when the examination results were announced. His pupils had done exceptionally well. Currie the teacher had arrived and he had every intention of staying. But once more Mason had other ideas, and again they would disrupt Currie's family and forge his future.

After James had completed a year at Keil, Mason informed him that a church at Coalburn, Lanarkshire, was looking for a minister.

The Scottish Forces' Magazine

Vol. 5. No. 2   February, 1945

THE LAND GIRL

PUBLISHED MONTHLY BY THE CHURCH OF SCOTLAND FOR SCOTS IN THE ROYAL NAVY, ARMY AND ROYAL AIR FORCE AND EDITED BY RONALD SELBY WRIGHT, S.C.F.

The forces' sweetheart. Peggy with Elsa *and* Jenny.

Peggy at Drumadoon.

Why didn't James apply? He promised that he would.

Why DID he apply?

'Because Mr Mason told me to.' There was no hesitation.

'I would have done anything for Mr Mason. I couldn't say no to him.'

But surely this was a major decision which would change not only his life, but that of his wife and, ultimately, his son?

'Yes. But Mr Mason told me to . . .'

Had he been considering returning to the pulpit?

'No, I was happy at Keil. I loved it, and the boys loved me. I was a good teacher – well, the boys did well in exams. I was playing rugby again and for the first time in my life I had money in my pocket. I almost had enough to put down a deposit on a house. Oh no, I was happy as a teacher . . .'

Currie was older, but he was still *agricola* to Mason the *magister*.

He preached at Coalburn, and was rejected by its vacancy committee. He was dejected and depressed. James Mason was not. There was a vacancy at Blawarthill, why didn't James apply for it? He did, he preached there, and he was rejected. The next kirk that Mason chose was in Irvine. It too, rejected the minister.

Three rebuttals would have all but broken the younger Currie but, fortified by the knowledge that his mentor was intent on him returning to the ministry, he scanned the Kirk's advertisements and applied for a vacancy at a church in Blackburn, West Lothian. It accepted him. However, Mason tells him that Blackburn is too far away from Keil. Currie tells the kirk there that he cannot become its minister. Without a thought of anything else, he applied for the vacancy because he thought James Mason wanted him to do so: without a thought for anything else, he rejected it because James Mason wanted him to do so.

How can this be explained? I do not attempt to do so. I simply state that it is so.

James Mason's next choice of church was more geographically suitable.

CHAPTER SIX

Memories of Millburn

'God decided before time began that this young man should be your minister.'

So said Professor Murdo Ewan MacDonald at James Currie's induction at Millburn Church in Renton. The 150 or so people present were further urged to 'take him, and take care of him.'

The powerful, earnest words underlined the dignity of the day, but Currie's ministry, which was to become synonymous with laughter, was about to start as it would continue. However the first punchline belonged to the Revd Dr James Martin, recently retired from High Carntyne, Glasgow, and his comment, Currie said with a twinkle in his eye, was the most important one he ever uttered.

Jim Martin told the congregation a little about their new minister and then, solemnly, he cautioned: 'But there is something I must tell you.' He paused for dramatic effect. Hands that strayed towards sweetie pokes froze; glances of surprises were exchanged; and folk leant forward eager to hear the confession.

'I must warn you that he is a . . . Rangers supporter!'

The revelation had the desired effect. There was a spontaneous cheer and the appreciation stopped just short of applause. Currie had arrived and the members of the congregation, many of them regulars at Ibrox stadium, went out of the kirk with joy in their hearts, eager to tell their friends about the new man.

James said: 'What a brilliant comment to make. It let the folk know right away that I was one of them, not another stuffed-shirt.'

The church roll at Renton listed 237 names, just enough to justify the appointment of a minister, although there had been talk of amalgamating Millburn with a neighbouring parish. When James set out to visit each of the members he discovered that about a hundred of them had 'either died and gone to heaven, or were spiritually dead.' The roll call was fairly typical of the following weeks, which consisted of promise, disappointment, and the quest to fulfill potential.

The manse at Millburn Road was an impressive red sandstone building which required only two things for restoration to its former

A pensive young James Currie.

glory – money and hard work. The latter the Curries would provide, the former was in short supply. When James and Peggy first saw the manse it had no electricity supply. Drumadoon Currie offered to fund its installation and be reimbursed when the church's finances were more healthy, but the kirk session would not hear of it. They worked their own little miracle and when the Curries moved in their first home in married life had been freshly decorated and electricity had been installed.

The spacious gardens had gone to seed. An overgrown tennis court was discovered at the foot of the grounds near the Balloch railway line. The challenge James faced was an old familiar one: reclamation of land and souls. He was prepared for the task. James Mason had reawakened his enthusiasm; and James knew that Peggy with young Jamesie would back him to the hilt. And so the parish work began – as laid down by Allan Easton. Visit the sick, visit the poor, visit the people in prison, help the needy.

His ministry began with one step forward and two back. The first setback was to the body of the kirk; the second to the spirit of its new custodian. Two days after James took over at Millburn the lead was stolen from the roof of the church hall. It appeared to James that there were roofs with lead all over Scotland, but this particular thief had chosen his roof at this particular time. Unfounded worries of persecution? On other occasions this charge would be justified, but this time the fears were not without foundation.

That same evening a minister from a neighbouring parish called on the Curries as they were sitting down to dinner. He declined an offer to share their food, said he could not even wait for a cup of tea, but he remained for two hours telling the young clergyman the magnitude of his 'impossible task at Millburn.' The previous minister, the Revd William Jeffrey, had been a 'brilliant man and even he could do nothing with the folk of the Vale of Leven.' They did not deserve a good minister. Currie's confidence sagged, then he discovered a spirit of defiance. He said: 'All this may be true, but perhaps you should have told me *before* my induction. I'm here now and I can only try.'

That minister did not realise it, but his words of gloom fired a fierce determination. Millburn was Currie's first time out on his own. At Drumadoon, Keil and West Pilton he had been 'second man', working under instruction and eager to seek advice and guidance. In Renton he was shouldering the responsibility, but fortunately his three senior office bearers were men of fortitude and strength.

John Blades, the session clerk, a tall, strapping man 'lived for Millburn Church.' Willie Graham, the treasurer, who was deaf, was a businessmen with United Company Red, and clerk to the congregational board, Charlie Craig was an engineer and union official at Dennie's shipyard. These three wise men had carried the kirk through its lean years, when unemployment in the Vale was high and faith was low. These men had chosen James Currie to lead the flock back to the folk. Setbacks were nothing new to them and, although the stolen lead amounted to a minor disaster, they assured their young minister it was simply another difficulty which would be resolved.

The church's funds had been bankrupted by the costs of installing electricity in the manse but, in the certain knowledge that 'God would provide', the hall roof was mended with copper.

Currie's first week in Renton was swallowed up 'electioneering'. He designed a handbill – 'I am your new minister and I will call at every house in the parish' – and took the text and a photograph of himself, snapped at an informal moment on Iona when he was wearing an open-necked shirt and his hair was tousled by the wind, to Willie McKelvie's printing shop near Renton cross. It was a visit which was to be repeated time and again as the advertising campaign began to pay dividends. The introductory offer pushed through letter boxes was fairly standard, but those which followed were more adventurous. One bill ordered, DON'T READ THIS, and it had the desired effect with one woman who raced after the minister.

'Ah wull sut read it,' she shouted.

She did, especially the smaller type which said . . . if you already come to church, please read it if you don't. The woman not only read it but came to the kirk to find out what it was about, liked what she heard, and remained a faithful attender.

Currie was following the Pilton principles and the people of the Vale began to follow him. Folk who had slipped away from the church returned; those who had been considering attending gave it a try; and others, caught up in the new wave of enthusiasm, went along to find out what it was all about. And they came back.

The Vale, too, was on the way back. The hammers' ding-dong echoed across the Clyde, the new factories – Burroughs, Westclox, Everlasting – brought jobs and prosperity. Families who had come through hard times during the depression and the war appreciated their better standard of living and many of the hands which were no longer idle also set to work for the kirk.

The Curries seemed to epitomise the fresh spirit sweeping through the area. Many of the men were working for the first time in their lives so they knew the difficulties the new minister was facing. Peggy, who went to work at the age of fourteen after the sudden death of her father, had much in common with the women folk. And young Jamesie? Well, a child can break the ice at a polar bears' convention.

The right man was in the right place at the right time. The pews were filling up and the church's overdraft, which was considerable, was no longer mounting. It was going so well James feared it was time for a comedown, and that happened while he was returning from visiting patients in Henry Brock Hospital. He was on the top deck of a bus. A drunk kept turning round to stare at him. The man knew the face, but his mind was so befogged by the Islay Mist that he couldn't put a name to it. Then it dawned, and he made his way unsteadily towards James and sat down beside him.

'You're the new minister.'

'Yes, I am.'

'Aye, I've seen your photy. Well, you should think black burnin' shame. A big strong man like you.'

James was shocked. 'What have I done?'

'It's what you huvnae done. Huv you seen the state of the cemetery. Black burnin' shame . . .'

And with that, he struggled down the stairs and got off the bus in indignation.

If the qualifications of the prosecutor were open to question his accusations were not. The graveyard was, indeed, in a poor condition. The grass was long and wild shrubs rose to six feet in some places. Taming the wilderness was to prove a demanding, arduous labour, but James took up a familiar tool, a scythe. and set to work with a will reclaiming the land. He did not have Johnny, the Drumadoon Clydesdale, to help but there was Jamesie, complete with sawn-off implements and mini-wheelbarrow.

About a month later, a degree of tidiness was achieved, but it was only a battle won in a perpetual war. Currie required reinforcements, so he mustered his reserves and bought a Qualcast motor mower from the quartermaster's store, otherwise known as the Co-op. Now he had the tools as well as the motivation – but defeat was looming in the shape of a persistent enemy – time, or to be strictly accurate, the lack of it. The demands of a flourishing parish were mounting and as James attended to them Mother Nature began to reassert herself at the cemetery. The contest was uneven, and it became evident that the rules would have to be changed. Those in charge of kirk graveyards throughout Scotland had encouraged similar problems and resolved them by passing over the maintenance to local authorities. Millburn kirk session recognised the wisdom of such a move and readily approved it. The decision was made easier by the quality of man who would take on the job.

Alex Smith was the superintendent of Cardross Cemetery, which sat on the slope of a brae with a glorious view across the vale to Bonhill. His graveyard had been chosen as one of the best-kept in the

The team that tamed the overgrown cemetery – James and Jamesie.

United Kingdom. Quite a contrast to Millburn. He expressed willingness to take on the duties and, with a sense of achievement, James wrote to the council to complete the formalities – or so he thought. The council replied that it would have been willing to take on the responsibility but it could not do so. An official explained that the law permitted councils to take over graveyards from parish churches, but Millburn, a former United Free Church, was not covered by the legislation. The county clerk at that time, Mr A A Templeton, saw a route out of the impasse. There was nothing in the law to prohibit Millburn from making a gift of the cemetery to the council, and no reason why the local authority should not accept it. This process was

duly carried out and Alex Smith's hard labours impressed everyone –
including the drunk on the top of the bus.

Alex Smith's choice of career was a strange one, particularly since
the cheery, little man was often taken to be a communist. Describing
his good work, Currie the master of the hyperbole waxes lyrical about
grass like a snooker table and flower beds with edges cut razor-sharp.
Smith was a practical, gentle man. He erected wire-netting around the
cemetery's flower beds to curtail the nocturnal visits of rabbits, but
the wire was a hindrance to them, not an insuperable barrier. 'I can't
bring myself to put up the tall netting – the rabbits have to live too.' He
became a regular visitor at the manse, although he was quick to
declare his beliefs, or rather, lack of them. He was a man of extreme
left-wing views, but definitely, James said, 'on the side of the angels'.
On the surface, this appears to be a convenient catch-all phrase,
providing an escape from a difficult situation. It is one James Currie
also used to describe his beloved poet Robert Burns, and he did not
offer it without due consideration.

Many of the men in the Vale were communists or, James said,
'thought they were'. Who could blame them? They had come through
times when four in five men were on the dole. Who had helped them?
What did they owe the Church? 'No, I couldn't blame them for being
disillusioned and in that disillusionment they turned to communism.'

Smith and Currie became great friends, and, although the little man
never indicated that he had amended his communist views, two
remarkable courses of events lead James to believe that he had. The
Iona Community advocated praying for the sick, and James carried
this out in his church, encouraging the congregation to mention
friends and relatives by name. One evening, much to the minister's
surprise and delight, Alex Smith appeared at a service. Later, he
explained that he had not attended for his own welfare, but had come
to pray for a friend's wife who was crippled by arthritis. Throughout
James's time in Renton the 'atheist' attended the church regularly.

'I don't know if Alex considered himself an atheist or agnostic, but I
do know that he was a man with a deep soul,' James said. 'I'm not one
for labels. I hate to hear about someone described as "a member of
this or that". A man's a man. The label doesn't matter. It's the man
underneath that's important.'

One winter's night in 1952 a car drew up at the manse at 11.00 pm. It
was Alex Smith with his rough-haired mongrel, Randy. Peggy was in
bed and it was obvious that James was also about to retire for the
night, but the little man accepted the offer of a cup of tea. He sat at the

kitchen table making small talk with the minister. He had something on his mind and eventually he got round to saying what it was. 'God's acre', as he called his cemetery in Cardross, had never been dedicated. He gazed at his hands, head bowed, and then he said: 'I think that's terrible.'

James concurred. 'Well, I'll be glad to do it.'

'Thanks,' Alex Smith said rising, 'let's do it now.'

So at midnight, under a dark, starless sky, the two friends and a mongrel stood on the slopes of the graveyard and a prayer was said to bless the hallowed ground, all those whose remains rested there, those who worked there, and the people who would be buried in the grounds. James Currie's astonishing memory flashed into instant recall and he described not only the drive to the cemetery and the still, blackness of the night but also the rough-haired 'Heinz' mongrel, its ear flapping forward as if it were smiling, scampering among the flower beds and uprooting some plants . . . 'and Alex said "wee Randy must have his fun too." Isn't that great? That's a man with a compassionate soul. Alex would have died for me and I think I would have tried to die for him . . .'

Although Alex Smith had at first been bemused by the bond of which had been forged between himself and a man of God, it did not surprise James Currie. His politics are now well known, advertised by marches in support of socialist causes and campaigns on behalf of the Labour Party in Scotland and a lifelong friendship with prominent politicians. Indeed, Bruce Millan, who was to become Secretary of State for Scotland, used the manse as his constituency 'home'. During the early years of his ministry James kept these views to himself, but that did not mean he was inactive politically, albeit working under-cover. And even to do that, he had to break a promise . . . a promise begged by his mother's cousin, a communist, and thorn in the flesh of the establishment.

Colin Currie was brought up in the shadow of the Duke of Montrose's castle on Arran, and many said that was where his extreme left-wing politics were born. As a boy, James saw the duke and duchess eating porridge at the kitchen table in Drumadoon and regarded them simply as friends of the family. However to Colin, the view from the other side of the castle walls was very different. His impression was that of a life of plenty, grandeur and privilege, while the ordinary folk had to struggle to survive. The name of Colin Currie became celebrated in some circles, notorious in others, for his battles in Glasgow and the West of Scotland. In the dark days of the depression, it was far from uncommon for families to run into debt. Warrant sales and evictions were commonplace – and so was the figure of Colin Currie, arguing for a better deal for the man in the street and opposing those trying to put him there.

Colin, of course, was well aware of James's socialist principles. When he heard that James was to take over at Millburn, Colin made his way to Drumadoon and there the communist tried to persuade the younger man to preach only the word of God and never to enter the arena of politics. James said that he would try to comply with his cousin's wishes but had to point out that there might be occasions when he believed the two were indivisible. When that occurred, he would have to say what he believed to be true, no matter the consequences.

Colin Currie, a skilled orator, tried all he knew to convince James that he must never dabble in politics. All of his arguments failed. Finally, in desperation, the communist got down on his knees and begged.

'Please James, give me your solemn promise – no politics. They've ruined me and they'll ruin you.'

They were the establishment.

James promised he would try to stay out of political issues, and it was a pledge he intended to keep. He believed, first and foremost, that a minister should represent the whole of his parish. That encompassed people of all political beliefs, so the minister must do nothing to put any barriers between the Church and its congregation.

Willie McKim, a Vale of Leven man, was one of Colin Currie's comrades. James met him early in his Millburn ministry and was told by one of his office bearers: 'Ye'll no' cut any ice wi' Willie McKim.' His belief in communism was staunch, and he had it written into his will that there should be no ministers at his funeral. However, it appeared that Colin had told his friend a bit about the new man at Millburn, and the two became great friends. Mrs McKim was a regular church attender and, as he entered the pulpit one day, James was delighted to see Willie beside her on the pew. Although he went to church only on a few occasions because, James said, 'he had bitter words to eat'. Willie McKim's views changed and James conducted his funeral service at Alex Smith's cemetery.

'It was a terrible day,' James said. 'The worst rain I've ever witnessed. We had to wait for a dry spell then bale out water from the grave before lowering the coffin. Willie McKim was a fine man. I was terribly sad when he died.'

The folk in the Vale felt the same way, and the unusual friendship did not go unremarked or unnoticed. The 'new man must have something,' they said, and many went to the kirk to find out what it was.

Another unlikely acquaintance put Currie in the public eye and did him no harm at all. The wife of a local who bent his elbow too much started to attend the church. James made a point of visiting the woman regularly, but never succeeded in meeting her husband. The man, we'll call him Tam, slipped out of the back door as the minister approached the front. Eventually James managed to meet the man and tried to persuade him to mend his ways. Tam, 'a harmless man, really', promised that he would try and he did, but always returned to the bottle.

He was well known to members of the local constabulary. The officers did not chase him to pay fines imposed in court for being drunk and disorderly. They knew that sooner or later Tam would go on a bender, and found it convenient to have a fine default outstanding against him so that they could offer a bed for the night and thus avoid a more unpleasant scene. A stay in a cell was a sobering experience. Hungover and contrite, Tam would be released in the morning with no charges being pressed.

One day the sergeant telephoned the manse. Tam had been drinking again and creating a disturbance in the street. If James could persuade him to return the bottle he had bought to the Helenslea Bar, the police would turn a blind eye. The minister went to the house and Tam, slurring his words, vehemently denied that he had any alcohol. His wife, however, produced a bottle of cheap wine. Tam feigned surprise, and agreed to take it back to the bar and get his money back. James thought this a fine idea, and willingly acted as support and escort.

As the workers poured out of Burroughs that evening they saw the local drouth and the minister stroll arm-in-arm into the Helenslea! The gossip raced through the Vale, closely followed by the facts. Here was a man who practised what he preached. They had seen his compassion; they came to Millburn to listen to him preach.

The parish boundary remained the same, but the scope of the church widened and its membership continued to grow. More members meant more visits, and James realised he would have to move with the times. The members of his flock were well scattered and the public transport system left much to be desired. Currie decided that he required to have his own form of transport so he could reduce travelling time and therefore increase the number and visits. A police officer was selling a bicycle. It would take all of the minister's savings, but one must speculate to accumulate . . . And so the minister became the proud owner of a second-hand pushbike – not just any bike but a big, sturdy beast of burden which turned out to be particularly prone to punctures. 'Have bike – will travel' was the new motto, with nothing to hold him back. Well, almost nothing, because cycles and Currie were a dangerous partnership. Twenty years previously, on the isle of Arran, a bicycle had almost been the death of James. Memories had faded of the jarring impact; pain; a slow, looping plunge over a bridge; then more pain followed by an enveloping watery darkness. However a few weeks after the acquisition of the policeman's bike, the incident came back vividly and painfully.

On Arran, the shy lad was known to his friends as 'The Minister'. In Renton, the minister leaving his manse and freewheeling the hundred yards downhill was for all the world like a big boy. It was like this one winter's evening as he set out to visit a parishioner. Dusk was falling and there was a gentle breeze on his back. The cycle sped downhill, gathering momentum rapidly, Currie steering nonchantly. Sunday's sermon had been on the subject of what followed pride, and it was about to be underlined painfully.

Almost at the foot of the hill, James noticed the telephone engineers at either side of the road. They had been working all day and were in the final stages of completing their task. The telephone wire they were raising was almost invisible in the failing light. It was a tripwire at neck-height when James hit it. Impact; pain; a crashing fall; more pain; and a cycle dented almost as badly as the minister's pride.

James repeated the story with glee, laughing heartily at himself, but the story also had a moral. The telephone cable hit him on the throat – exactly on his clerical collar. Just before the point of impact, the engineer's spotted the dare-devil cyclist, saw that a collision was inevitable, and released the strain on the wire. The end result was another Currie story, oft repeated, but it could have had tragic consequences.

'It just goes to prove that with God's protection and a little commonsense we can come through the most difficult situations.'

The cycling clergyman became a familiar figure in the Vale. From the saddle, he could watch what was happening in the community and, equally important, he was seen by the people, 'salt of the earth folk who did not suffer fools gladly but respected a man who worked for his living.' Currie was now well in the latter category.

One day, a tremendous explosion reverberated along the Vale. A compression chamber had burst at the Royal Navy torpedo factory in Alexandria. The blast caused widespread damage. Benches and tools were sent flying and part of the roof were smashed by debris. One man was killed and four were seriously injured. A fleet of ambulances raced to the scene from Dumbarton and Alexandria. Every available doctor in the district was called and emergency operations were carried out to release workers trapped in the rubble.

Fearing the worst, James jumped on to his cycle and hurried to the scene. He arrived with the emergency services. One workman, his face blackened by smoke, turned to a colleague and said: 'See, I told you. If Currie's no' here already he's on his way.' James did not know the man, but he knew his message had got through to him. A minister must be with the people when they need him.

Around this time James gained the invaluable services of a shy, caring man whose name can now be revealed. Mr Oswald, who was out walking his dog, stopped the minister in the street and introduced himself.

'I could have done with your help a few years ago,' he said.

His son had been on HMS Hood which had been hit by the Germans during the Second World War. A shell had gone down her funnel and exploded in the heart of the vessel. Mr Oswald's son was one of the many lives lost. The father remembered all too clearly the feeling of despair and desolation he had struggled to conquer. He had not wanted to burden any friends or members of his family with his own grief. He had learned to live with his loss, and in time his faith had been strengthened. Nevertheless, he had often longed for a talk with a compassionate companion, and the young man at Millburn was rapidly earning that reputation. Mr Oswald had determined that in a quiet, unassuming way he would attempt to help others facing similar grief. He said there was not much a simple man could do, but he kept his eyes and ears open and could tell James of people who needed his assistance.

One fine, summer day Mr Oswald told James about a girl in Killearn Hospital. Jean Melvin was just fifteen years old but had undergone a major brain operation. Her convalescence would be long and wearing. Could the minister find time to visit the girl? That same day, James mounted his trusty bike and cycled the ten miles or so to the hospital. The girl was delighted to see him and his jokes were just the tonic she needed. The minister spoke to the other patients and, before setting off for home, had another chat with Jean. She said that

59

as soon as she got home she would come to see him. James promised they would eat strawberries and ice cream on the lawn. And that promise gave her a goal.

The following Sunday James stood at the kirk door after morning service, shaking hands with the members of the congregation. He noticed a small, stout woman dallying, obviously waiting until the church was empty so she could talk to him. James had noticed her in the kirk, although she was not a member of Millburn. The woman was Jean Melvin's mother. When the crowd had dispersed Mrs Melvin came forward and took James by the hand. With tears in her eyes, she thanked him for going to all that trouble to visit her daughter.

Then she said: 'If that's the kind of man you are I'll come to your church. Oh, I've said I'd come before, but it's for real this time.'

It certainly was for real. Mrs Melvin attended Millburn faithfully, and soon came the proud day when her daughter, after eating strawberries and ice cream at the manse, sat beside her on the pew, completely recovered from her delicate operation. In the coming weeks, they persuaded other members of the family to come along. The numbers around mother and daughter continued to swell as Mrs Melvin, a marvellous disciple, told her story to friends and neighbours. Her joy was contagious, and young Jean appeared to be living proof of the new life the family was enjoying.

Mrs Melvin was a recruiting officer *par excellence*. As she told folk what the minister had done for her daughter, what the church was doing for her was gloriously obvious. And people wanted to share it.

The children of the Melvin family joined the Sunday School. The older ones entered Bible Class and Youth Fellowship. The women came to the Guild. Menfolk joined the Christian industrial council James had just set up.

One day James and Peggy worked out the number of people brought to the church, directly and indirectly, by Mrs Melvin.

The total was more than one hundred!

Currie's ministry was working. Mrs Melvin was an example of the Iona Community's belief that the Church is a living organism. It belongs to the people – it *is* the people. Like a plant given the proper care and nourishment it will flourish and grow. The dark days of West Pilton seemed so far away. The dejected, despairing man who turned his back on the pulpit was now reaping the rewards of those demanding years which had come so close to breaking him. And the rewards were drawn from the same disciplines which the young man had found so harrowing.

'I was hammered out on the anvil,' James said. 'Allan Easton almost broke me. But he made me.'

One of James Currie's greatest assets was that he liked people. If this statement appears trite, consider how many people you genuinely like and then assess how many of those you would still like if they came to your home night after night, week after week, to tell you their troubles and woes. When would they cease to be friends and begin to be tiresome, tedious and a downright nuisance. I would not run out of fingers counting. James was special. He was happy to count everyone from Rhubarb Roots to the Earl of Elgin as friends. And most of that large number came to him in foul weather.

One Saturday morning he was enjoying a leisurely breakfast in the manse. It was a fine, sunny day and he was looking forward to going to Keil to referee a rugby match. There was a knock on the door, and when James answered it he came face to face with a young man whose name frequently came up in conversation in the manse although he had never seen the inside of Millburn Church.

Trying to conceal his surprise, James asked Hamish to come in, but the young man declined. He was troubled, and he did not want to set foot in the manse. He would tell his story on the doorstep, in his own time.

'I'm getting married,' he said eventually.

'Now that's just super,' Currie enthused, a great believer in a good woman sorting a man out. He waited patiently to be asked to tie the knot.

Hamish confessed: 'She's a Catholic and she's divorced. Her family's against it. We're getting married today in the Registrar's Office.'

James tried to reassure the man that if they worked hard at their marriage and lived a decent life everything would be all right. In fact, he admired him for having the courage and obvious love to go ahead.

Still, there was a sadness in the young man. Head bowed, he mumbled what had been worrying him so deeply.

'I've got no shoes.'

Involuntarily, James looked down and saw that Hamish was wearing scruffy boots, hardly fitting footwear for a bridegroom. Currie had no money, so he took off his own shoes and handed them to Hamish. They were size eight and a half, too big for the smaller man, but with toilet paper stuffed into the toes they fitted the bill.

Although Hamish was not a church attender, the minister knew him well. Six times in three years, James had visited him in Barlinnie. His convictions had all been for theft. On one occasion Peggy's brother, Police Inspector Hector McLean, spotted an intruder on a factory roof and crept up on him. It was Hamish, busily removing lead. Hector shone the torch on the young man's face.

Hector said with what could have been a glint of a smile: 'It's a fair cop, sur.' Then his face took on a worried look and he said: 'Please don't tell Mr Currie.'

Currie, of course, was told and after Hamish had been returned to Barlinnie the minister again went to see him. As he followed a prison officer along the foreboding corridors, past cells that held persistent offenders, it suddenly became depressingly clear that he had walked the route before, could do so again, and not make a blind bit of difference. Obviously nothing he had said or done in the past had persuaded Hamish to mend his ways, and he had nothing fresh to say. Feelings of inadequacy began to well up and, unwittingly, he gave voice to his thoughts. His concern was not just about Hamish, not even about prison visiting, but Currie's confidence was low. He was having doubts about his ability as a minister.

'I'm wasting my time,' he mumbled.

The inside of the prison was still and the walls seemed to take the words and throw them back louder.

The prison officer stopped quickly, spun and wheeled round.

'Don't say that! Don't ever say that again. We can say it; the police can say it; but the minister is the man who must never give up.'

The minister's mind flashed back to the boulder in the Doon field and he heard his father's voice: 'You're not going to give up now, James.'

I wondered if, with a good woman behind him, Hamish became a man fit to fill a minister's shoes.

James smiled as he said: 'Oh well, after he got married he didn't go to prison . . .'

There was a pause.

'. . . so much.'

Success is relative.

Hamish was not the young man's name. Since James Currie's ministry was about people, indeed his life revolved around others, it is impossible to attempt to present some understanding of the man without telling about the folk he helped. Many of the people he described with affection were, in his words, 'black sheep'. Excise them from these pages and the volume becomes very much thinner. Every family has its skeleton in the cupboard, and it is not the purpose of this book to exhume them. Then is no intention to embarrass or offend. James was a well-read, articulate man and, according to many of his peers, a learned theologian and a deeply spiritual minister. He could hold his own with the finest brains at the General Assembly of the Church of Scotland, but his sermons were never 'heavy'. He was not one for flowery phrases, and his meaning was unmistakable. In a newsletter to members of his congregation he said that church officers would call at every home to discuss problems and criticised those who had not been attending the kirk. But he put it better: 'Let's cut the cackle. We cannot go on with dead-heads masquerading as Christians.' He wanted his story to be told, not for vainglorious reasons because he knew that he would, once more, stand accused of being the 'big head', but so that his style of ministry, the parish system, might perceive more consideration and perhaps be adopted more widely. The parish system, put simply, is caring for every person in the parish. These pages are filled with stories of some of those people. Identities, locations and dates have been altered in many cases to safeguard anonymity and honour confidence. But the essence of the stories are as James told them.

David is one man who appreciates Currie's style.

The minister was a fervent believer in visiting schools as often as possible. Children can be intimidated and overawed by a church: the big, imposing exterior; inside cold stone and wood; scrubbed hands and stern faces; stiff backs; and glowers that demand absolute silence. Sundays can take on the spectre of penance with must be suffered with resolution. The classroom is informal, much less inhibiting, and it is the children's home ground. The minister is going to *them*. James, who always strived for a relaxed atmosphere in church, relished school visits. The child in him, which was always bursting to get out, spoke to them, laughed longer than they did, and they paid him the ultimate compliment by treating him as an equal. His talks were always bursting with anecdotes and stories. The Bible was not a book of 'thou shalt nots', but a constant source of adventure, joy and miracles. He left the child with the story to come to his own conclusions. He hated the conventional, seemingly mandatory, and the moral is this . . .

'One wee girl went home and said to her mum "I love Mr Currie – he has no morals".'

The children looked forward to his visits. The barrier was broken, the link forged, and the steps of the church lead to the home of an old friend. Sundays were an extension of the relaxed chats in school.

Suffer little children to come unto me was a Currie favourite. And he was a favourite of the children.

But when he was in the classroom, he was watching. Potential elders were spotted there. One such lad, George, had all the qualities, but much to James's disappointment he showed no interest in the kirk. After the boy left school, James did not see him for about a year, then he caught sight of him in the street and got off his bike to chat. The youth had matured and was serving an apprenticeship in the shipyards. But he was withdrawn, embarrassed to be seen talking to the minister.

Finally, James broached his topic: 'Why won't you come to church?'

George tried to avoid the question, but the minister persisted.

'Is it something I've said? Something I've done? Please tell me.'

'No, it's nothing. It's . . . nothing.'

'But I'd love you to come to church. Won't you try?'

'I can't.'

'Of course you can. What is there to stop you?'

With a sadness beyond his years, but one which had haunted him since childhood, George replied: 'I can't because *my name stinks.*'

He'd said it, and it was only then that James realised that the lad's father was a drunkard who spent more time inside prison than out of it. He had never associated the boy with the man. The sins of the father had been visited upon the son: a blameless son who felt stained and debased by the stigma.

The story ends happily. George was persuaded that there was life for him in the church if he had a place for the church in his life. He could do nothing to alter what his father had done or how other folk might look on his actions. But he could fashion his own way of life and force those some critics to see him as his own man.

'And what a fine man,' James said.

He fulfilled Currie's early expectations and is now a church elder and a father of whom his own sons are proud. George learned that name and reputation are given by others. Respect is earned, and is infinitely more valuable.

CHAPTER SEVEN

A week in life

Spirits at Millburn were much higher and the fabric of the kirk reflected this. Its rebirth, coinciding with the words of a drunk, began at the cemetery with the minister/farmer swinging a scythe. Once more the graveyard was discussed on the buses but now the words were complimentary. Peggy had turned the manse into a home, the first she and her husband had had to themselves. A modest stipend, substantially below the amount James earned as a teacher, meant that cash was in short supply, but careful budgeting and gifts from family and friends allowed them to furnish it comfortably.

James had been busy taming its overgrown gardens. Weeds were banished and shrubs and flowers flourished. The tennis court had been rescued, and resounded to the laughter of children.

The copper which had replaced the stolen lead on the church hall was weathering green. It had withstood the worst of the weather and unwelcome attention of thieves.

The congregation, the heart of Millburn, was healthy and the body was shaping up nicely. Larger attendances brought in extra funds. The overdraft was steadily being eroded and the day was not far off when it would be eradicated altogether. All was going well, until . . .

A structural engineer examining the church on a routine visit found that its spire was in a dangerous condition. He had no choice but to condemn it. The cost of repairs was frightening. It was with a gloomy heart that James Currie reported the gravity of the situation to his kirk session. There was silence as each man considered the implications. Then Willie Graham spoke.

'If it must be done, it must be done.'

A simple statement.

'But the money . . .? Currie countered.

'Don't worry about the money,' Graham reassured him. 'God will provide.'

It did not seem humanly possible that a congregation the size of Millburn could raise the hundreds of pounds required. Not humanly possible, perhaps, but Willie Graham had faith.

James speaking at a fête in the manse gardens, Renton.

The work was done and paid for. James was not sure where the money came from; certainly, there were no large contributions from wealthy benefactors, no windfalls or strokes of good fortune. The living organism in Renton responded to the emergency. Responded magnificently.

The trim gardens at the manse were utilised to hold fetes, which paid a double dividend. They provided profit and brought people into contact with the members of the church. There were no stiff backs and glowers demanding silence, it was fun, laughter and brotherhood. Renton people liked what they saw in Millburn people. And Renton people became Millburn people. Currie the conductor was happy to see church members perform the work . . . and the audience's eagerness to join the orchestra. As they continued to play in harmony, it released James to continue the work.

What is a minister's work?

A popular view is that he works one day a week, Sunday, with the occasional call-out to weddings and funerals. He doesn't have to clock-in or out; has no gaffer; no production target to meet. As an example of a week in the life of James Currie, here are some extracts from his diary:

1 February 1953: 11.30 am; morning service; Sunday School; Youth Fellowship; evening service; 'Our hearts are sad because of the sinking yesterday of Princess Patricia in Irish Sea. 134 missing. Floods in England and Holland. Hundreds drowned.' Six visitors at the manse in the evening.

2 February: Sawed up fallen tree in garden; three telephone calls from people seeking assistance and advice; telephoned session clerk about church business; telephoned Mr Mason at Keil; called at Woman's Guild at 9.15 pm; early to bed.

3 February: Presbytery meeting; six telephone calls; meeting of Cadets – request to become chaplain approved; wrote four letters; made three visits; attended Deacon's Court for election of new deacons; annual business meeting; 10.00 pm, more telephone calls.

4 February: Wrote four letters; five telephone calls; visited by mother of man in Barlinnie; took funeral service; conducted film show at church hall; visited three parishioners. Asked today to be one of the leaders in 'Tell Scotland' campaign.

5 February: Cut logs from fallen tree; wrote three letters; visited Henry Brock Hospital; spoke at Guild of Friendship; conducted wedding ceremony; made seven visits; attended fund-raising meeting from 9.15 pm until midnight.

6 February:: Terribly tired; wrote two letters; visited ten people; baptised boy; attended pantomime rehearsal at church hall.

7 February: Worked on sermon and tidied study; wrote two letters; made five visits; Mr and Mrs Mason called at manse; worked on sermons for a long time.

Hardly a one-day-week job. Obviously, no two weeks are the same, but 1-7 February 1953 was selected because it was fairly typical of how James Currie spent his time at Renton. The factor which must always be borne in mind is that most people who telephone or come to see a minister are experiencing some kind of difficulty, be it spiritual, mental or physical. James believed in sharing these problems and that put a tremendous strain on him. One minister I spoke to put the burden into perspective: 'One day after visiting fourteen people I had to go home. I was mentally exhausted. Can you imagine trying to listen to fourteen potted histories of fourteen families and then trying to offer advice and guidance? There's only so much you can take. James Currie was a phenomenon. I honestly don't know how he took it all.'

James kept a large desk diary all his days, filling it in faithfully each night, or in the early hours of the morning, before he went to sleep. It was not just a list of his duties and record of events, but a confidante which received modest information of successes and elaborate descriptions of failures and criticism. The first week of February 1953, is remembered by the shipping disaster, Scotland's defeat on the rugby field and a number of important events in his ministry at Millburn. The diary might have belonged to any minister of the church. But could it have been written by any married man with two young sons? There is no mention of wife or family. In that week, in fact in almost every week, James Currie had little time to give to his family. When he went on to St James, Pollok, that little time became less. He writes of his sons 'suddenly growing up', and in later years realises that he missed their childhood and caught fleeting glimpses of their youth. The Church came first. The man who loved children saw little of his own.

CHAPTER EIGHT

Political undertones

Renton had a flourishing corps of Cadets which did not have a chaplain and this provoked a crisis of conscience for James Currie, a committed pacifist. The corps was well run and an excellent means of teaching the lads of the Vale the value of discipline, but he saw it as a training ground for the armed services: the boys, fodder for the fields of war. He also believed passionately that the minister must go where the people are and, after wrestling with the dilemma for months, he decided that he could defend his principles from afar or reconnoitre and try to help the boys. In February 1953, he was appointed chaplain to the corps. Another forward thrust for the army of the Lord.

The most immediate and obvious result of this was an increase in attendance at Millburn's youth organisations. The door had been opened and the minister had given them an insight into what lay beyond. They entered eagerly. But this relatively minor event had a tremendous effect on Currie himself. He had bent a little, sacrificed a principle, and it was good for his church; it was good for the people. There was criticism from some fellow ministers but he came out of it all knowing he had done the right thing. The happy man had a happy, thriving congregation, now the pragmatist was about to enter other spheres and open doors in his broad kirk.

The folk of the Vale had come through hard times and would not easily forget it. A goodly proportion of their councillors, including the man who represented James's ward, were communists, 'hard-working, enthusiastic men,' who were re-elected time after time. The success of these men stuck in Currie's craw.

'If they won a victory it was not just for the people but for the communist cause,' he said. 'I knew we had good men in the church, men of great principles, and that they could strike a blow for us.'

Us, was the Church and the Labour Party.

Currie was well aware of the dangers of becoming involved in politics – 'Promise me, James, no politics – they'll ruin you' – but he wanted to break the mould. His clandestine entry into the political arena might have been thwarted had he married 'a suitable wife', and those are Peggy's words, but Margaret Flora MacLean Currie cannot be described as the conventional woman in the manse. Her father died when she was fourteen and she lied about her age to join the land army so she could send money home to her mother to help support her younger brothers Donald and Tearlach. Her socialist views were formed early and she did not believe in hiding them. Together they developed a strategy. They nurtured church members with similar views and encouraged them to stand for office. When the elections came along two men covertly coached by the Curries were elected to the council. The communist stranglehold had been broken. And James was convinced that he had done the right thing.

There were not many people who even suspected the minister's role in the affair, but one of the few remaining communists had an inkling. One day the councillor and James appeared on the same platform at an industrial tribunal, arguing for the reinstatement of two men who had been dismissed from a shipyard for refusing to clean an oil sump unless they were provided with protective clothing. Much to the councillor's chagrin, James was asked by the chairman of the tribunal to speak first. He argued convincingly that the man he was representing was of impeccable character and his record at work, regarding both discipline and attendance, was beyond reproach. He had not refused to carry out the task, he had simply asked for industrial clothing to enable him to do it efficiently and safely. If this were provided, and surely any reasonable employer would be willing to do so, he would be only too happy to let bygones be bygones and return to work to clean the oil sump.

Case proven. Worker reinstated. Clothing to be provided. Next.

Counsel for the defence had led evidence so skilfully that the verdict in the second case was a foregone conclusion. The councillor was warming to his rhetoric when the chairman interrupted him.

'Thank you, but we've heard enough.'

His 'client' was reinstated on the same terms. The communist, his case won but his thunder stolen, raced after Currie in an attempt to re-establish the pecking order.

'See you,' he said reproachfully, 'you'll never be as good as me before tribunals because you've got to tell the truth. If it suits my case I can tell lies.'

Up till now it had been convenient for Currie to be economical with the truth about his political leanings. He was a minister and had to be careful not to alienate church members of other persuasions, so he contented himself with making the balls and letting Peggy fire them.

However a demonstration in St Andrew's Halls, Glasgow, went a long way towards putting his beliefs into the public domain. The meeting was called to protest against the Central African Federation, which had been imposed against the will of the blacks on that continent. It was an overtly political gathering, but conscience (not to mention Peggy) persuaded James that he must attend. He was not the only minister to do so, but, he said, he was the only one from his parish. The Curries' appearance at the protest against inequality and injustice was the first of many. Some of his members were openly hostile over his stance, but the majority of the folk in the Vale applauded it and respected him for it.

The 'ordinary guy' was never far from the mood of the people and, reluctantly, he was having to concede one common factor in attracting fresh faces to the pews. The novelty value of the new man had long since departed yet the roll was continuing to rise. The main reason for this was the hard work put in by the church officials and the congregation itself, but there was another element which Currie could no longer ignore. He got closer to the people, and they came closer to the kirk, when he was simply himself, when he acted on his gut feelings. The young man who ate his sandwiches in the lavatory because he was afraid his fellow students would laugh at anything he had to say was now centre stage, listening to cries of encore. He had, of course, put out photographs and leaflets when he arrived in Renton but that was simply advertising material, no more than clever marketing. And he was selling the Church. Now Currie found himself a major attraction, and decided 'if that's what they want that's what they will get', even though it went against the grain.

Those who loved the entertainer's offerings at Burns Suppers or after-dinner speeches; those who loathed his frequent appearances on television, radio and the columns of newspapers might be interested to know that the Currie high-profile was born when a conscientious objector walked into the wooden hut of a Cadets' corps.

Currie's passion for football was matched by that of the Renton folk and the local junior team, Vale of Leven, were giving them lots of excitement. Although it meant foregoing trips to Ibrox to see his beloved Glasgow Rangers, James went to see the Vale whenever possible. They progressed comfortably through the early rounds of the Scottish Junior Cup, and Currie became something of a lucky mascot. So much so, that there was disappointment when he said that he could not attend an away match because he had to visit church members who were in hospital. But the supporters were not prepared to lose their talisman, so their bus made an unscheduled stop at the Western Infirmary, Glasgow, and, while James visited the sick, the team duly dispensed with their opponents. Currie was able to attend the remaining cup matches and was on the terraces of Scotland's national stadium, Hampden, to see the Vale lift the cup. One disgruntled opposition fan was later heard to mumble: 'What chance did we have? Their ------- minister was praying for them.'

The following day James took the cup into the pulpit: 'There is a trophy laid up in heaven for those who triumph in the name of the Lord . . .' There were some who criticised this common touch: many more who found that the kirk had a meaning in their everyday lives.

Currie's magic touch was also well to the fore when he started a pantomime. Much of the banter was at the expense of members of the congregation and the minister/producer wrote several lines poking fun at himself. To set the mood of the show, he appeared as the devil. Between scenes on the opening night one of the audience remarked: 'The auld devil's great, isn't he?'

Young Charles piped up: 'That's my dad. He's the auld devil!'

The idea had been fun and fellowship, but, to James's surprise, it proved a great financial success. And, perhaps, a success on a more commercial footing. Mrs Robertson, a Rentonian, asked the minister if she could have a copy of the script. She explained that her son-in-law was about to appear in pantomime and was always on the look-out for fresh ideas. James was happy to oblige. Later that month he went to see how the professionals put on a show and was flattered to discover that some of his jokes had been used in the production. Mrs Robertson was there to see her son-in-law, a young man called Stanley Baxter. No one enjoyed that show more than James Currie. He laughed often and he laughed loudly because he well knew the therapeutic value. And he knew the wisdom in Sean O'Casey's words: 'In the midst of life we are in death . . . in the midst of death we are in life.' The old year was ending with tears of joy. The new one was to bring tears of grief.

James went to West Pilton, where his ministry began and all but ended, to speak at a youth club. While he was there he got the news that James Mason had suffered a coronary thrombosis. Two days later, he died.

It was Easter. The time of death and resurrection.

Mason had been one of the major influences in Currie's life. He accepted the raw lad from Arran and produced the leader of the college. He led the youth into the rose garden and emerged with the

Currie twists again at a pantomime in Renton.

young man yearning for the pulpit. He took the broken minister who had fled to the plough back to Keil and set the course for a wiser man to take up the reins at Millburn. James Mason knew James Currie: understood his strengths and weaknesses. Where Drumadoon had tried the iron fist to make a man of his son Mason handled the boy with a velvet glove. After the demands of Allan Easton's parish had sapped strength and confidence, he nurtured the young man's belief in himself and his true vocation. The bond between the two was broken, temporarily. Twenty-four years later James Currie died after suffering a coronary thrombosis.

It was Easter. The time of death and resurrection.

CHAPTER NINE

Success and failure

All his life, James Currie trod a tightrope. Those who loved, or loathed, the extrovert entertainer who was so confident at the microphone, will find it difficult to believe that behind the mask was a man haunted by self-doubt. He was afraid that he would be 'found out'. Even when he was in his sixties, with decades of satisfied audiences behind him, he waited for the shepherd's crook to snatch him off the stage.

His success in the pulpit was regarded in the same way: the 'ordinary guy' who enjoyed the acclaim had a poor opinion of himself. He feared that others must surely arrive at this view. Always, the fears manifested themselves at times of triumph. When he had been working hard, and the rewards were evident, the doubts that he was unworthy would well up. The insecurities of West Pilton were never far from the surface.

Currie's work in May 1953, would be a source of pride to any minister in the Church of Scotland. His policy of going to meet the people, then bringing them to the Church, was really working. These extracts from his diary are evidence of that.

6 May: Sang at Men's Club social and prize-giving. Peggy presented prizes.

7 May: Communicants' class at manse; Dramatic Club meeting; meeting of Scottish Christian Industrial Organisation.

8 May: Meeting with coronation festivity groups; went with MacArthur's lorry with one hundred and five cups and thirty-six saucers to Joint Hospital for fête.

9 May: Cycled to Joint Hospital for fête.

10 May: Decided on Intercession Group and Parish Register.

11 May: Tell Scotland meeting; visits to Barlinnie and hospitals.

12 May: Attracted attention of press – two reporters from *People's Journal* called.

13 May: Progress on foundations of new hall.

14 May: Attended the launch of Arcadia – 'wonderful but cold'; visited Western Infirmary; conducted baptism.

15 May: Went to county buildings with plans for hall; took stencil to Dewrance via Hiram Walker's; at opening of Drama Club.

16 May: Six o'clock reveille; went to county planning department; on to electricity board with plans.

19 May: 'Great day' at General Assembly of Church of Scotland; Peggy in Moderator's Gallery; 'lovely tea and supper' at Mrs Adamson's at West Pilton.

20 May: Had to leave Assembly to conduct funeral service in Renton; (back to Edinburgh in evening and reflects): 'Were the years in West Pilton wasted? NO. A seed sown is never wasted entirely, and this was my training ground. I have a great deal to be grateful for.'

21 May: Very good day at Assembly; impressions of day (a) a great opportunity which may depart; (b) we must not waste our chance; (c) let us concentrate on essentials; (d) prayer need not be long to be effective.

22 May: Highlight of the day was hearing the Revd Cameron Peddie speak on spiritual healing at well-attended meeting in Tolbooth Kirk. He is a most consecrated man, utterly devoted to the Lord.

23 May: Dinner with Fred Smith (another spiritual healer); Vale of Leven won cup.

24 May: Back at Millburn; first meeting of Prayer Group.

27 May: Attended old folks' concert; went to Auchterarder on bus trip with Dramatic Club.

28 May: Took funeral service which was attended by many Roman Catholics and members of Communist Party; good attendance at Social Club.

29 May: Very busy day preparing for tomorrow's fête in manse garden; evening in manse with at least thirty-five others getting ready for fête.

30 May: 'Well, the fête is over. Time is 12.40 am. We were up at 8.00 am and I haven't stopped even for a minute all day. Some people have the brass neck to say that ministers don't work! We made £100 or so – but the value of the day is not purely financial. It must also be measured in terms of happiness, which people had. The sun made up its mind about 2.00 pm and shone well for us. Ian McColl (the Rangers' footballer who opened the fête) was ideal, along with his wife and baby, Ian. We had a lot of good workers and they deserve every praise. Dad, James and Iris, who did a lot of service in her little Renault car, arrived about 11.00 am. I visited Dumbuie Avenue, Joint Hospital, and places for pictures. Our painting display was really first-class, though we made only 70/- at it. We had three ponies. The concert tonight was excellent. All did extremely well. It's a great life – if you don't weaken!

31 May: Good attendance at Sunday services; Cadets' parades to morning service; very smart; tired tonight – as usual.

James Currie could not accept his own success. At the beginning of June, life was great – but he weakened; mentally, more than physically. He wrote that his 'feeling of dejection and despair can hardly be described.'

On 2 June 1953 the Queen was crowned. James had been involved in arranging coronation festivities in Renton and that day he painted on his happy face and attended three parties. However, after the greasepaint had been removed, he told his diary his impressions of the day: 'How lonely the Queen looked – e.g. kneeling at the altar: how like is life to a firework – a frenzied flash of brilliance then it fizzles out; the music was wonderful, yet some did not like it.' Then came the introspection: 'One's point of view does not count.'

James did not know the reason why he became so depressed. He recognised, in later life, that he was vulnerable after a period of accomplishment. He said: 'Perhaps I saw what could be done and when I fell short of that I became frustrated . . . or maybe it was just a reaction to working too hard. I really don't know. It just sort of happened.'

At these times Peggy offered support and comfort. She had seen the effects of depression early in life when her mother was menopausal.

'I swore I would never become like that,' she said, 'but I recognised what James was going through. He never really got over his breakdown in West Pilton. Perhaps I should have stood up to him at the start: been firm and tried to shake him out of it. But there's no sense in saying "thou shalt not go into a depression" because there's nothing you can do about it.'

On Monday, 1 June, James was awakened early by a visitor to the manse. In the forenoon he planted potatoes (Arran Peaks) and cut grass with a scythe. In the afternoon he conducted a funeral (nearly all those attending were Roman Catholics); visited the homes of four parishioners; bought nemesia and antirrhinum from a nursery; and returned to the Community Centre the pictures which had been borrowed for display at the fete. He took a service at 8.00 pm., then planted the flowers in his garden until after 11.00 pm.

The following day he put on a happy face for the coronation festivities, and Wednesday was devoured by visiting nine patients in the Western Infirmary, eight at Henry Brock Hospital, and attending to the problems of nine people who called at the manse. Thursday was another busy day when he was completely 'washed out. As dead as a dodo and as pale as a whitewashed wall.'

The pattern of ensuring that every waking moment was occupied continued and, on 9 June, it appeared to have worked when he had a 'glorious day of sunshine, happiness and laughter' with 260 folk from Renton on their outing to Crieff, Callander and Aberfoyle.

However Thursday brought hours of 'scivvying in the kitchen' and Friday saw him 'in the depths of a deeper depression than I've known for many a long day.' Good performances at the Drama Club's show, Midsummer Madness, on three evenings the following week did nothing to lift the shroud of gloom, but a healthy breeze was drifting from the west, from his beloved Iona.

James had a working holiday there at the end of June, and it worked wonders to restore his confidence and enthusiasm for life. He was in charge of a group of slaters, ensuring slates were safely unloaded from a ketch, transported without damage, and firmly fixed to roofs. He enjoyed being part of a team effort, but still a little in melancholy mood noted that a chain is only as strong as its weakest link.

Early in June, Currie was off to another camp, refreshed and rejuvenated. He went with the Cadets to Woodhouselee, Midlothian. Rain beat down on the tents, the wind rattled through the trees, but he records the bliss of being snug in his bed. There is disappointment when Padre's Hour is cancelled to make way for a demonstration on how to blow up a mansion – 'what a horrible thing war is', – but the trip and connection with the Cadets is rated as a success.

All through the days of insecurity James leant on Peggy. But she received little support from him.

'Nothing could interfere with James's work,' she said. 'Many, many times I wished it could be otherwise. But now I know he was right. When I look back I've no regrets. I'm very proud of him and what he achieved. I'd do it all over again.

Peggy's health had not been good. Charles's birth had complicated, necessitating weeks of recuperation in hospital. Back problems had required a further spell of hospitalisation. At the beginning of July, 1953, she contracted dysentery, and, later that month she laboured through a severe throat infection. The illness became acute and the effects of the poison coursing through her system once more forced her back to bed.

James's diary records on Sunday, 26 July: 'Peggy's throat burst but she is still not well.'

In fact, while he had been taking morning service, Peggy had been alone in the manse vomiting poison so violently that she was afraid she would choke. While his wife was still confined to bed, James Currie went with the Revd Fred Smith to perform the 'laying on of hands', a spiritual healing ceremony, on a parishioner.

That same day, Peggy's sister, Catriona, and her husband, Jim Allison, one of the elders at Millburn, arrived at the manse. Catriona was the district nurse based at Luss, and saw immediately the seriousness of Peggy's condition. When James came home, Jim Allison gave him a piece of his mind. Currie was nonplussed. He was not heartless, but he had taken Peggy for granted. He was so wrapped up in the work of his parish that he had not noticed how ill his wife was. His diary records that Jim Allison 'seems to think I'm some kind of ogre who mistreats his wife.'

Attempting to explain the 'misunderstanding', James said: 'Peggy was ill and I was sorry for her, but there was nothing I could do for her. How could I tell people I couldn't come to see them because my wife was ill. Peggy understood that.'

Did she understand, or did she feel neglected?

'A bit of both,' she said. 'But that was just the way James was, the way he'd always been.'

CHAPTER TEN

The prison pastor

Visit the people in prison.

This Easton edict would, on the surface, appear to offer least chance of success. Admittedly, it provided a captive audience, but hardly one in a suitable frame of mind to count blessings.

Peggy's Aunt May and Uncle John lived at Carmyle, and James would go there about once a month as a launching pad for visits to Barlinnie. He became a well-known face and on one occasion as he walked with the governor through the yard while the prisoners were exercising so many inmates spoke to the minister that the governor said: 'You're better known in here than me.' James Currie was proud of that comment.

If it was Inspector MacLean's job to ensure that deserving cases from the Vale were sent down for a stay at Her Majesty's expense, Currie saw it as his task to try to prevent a return visit. On one occasion the in-laws combined to have a man jailed – and that proved to be the foundation of a lucrative and legal career.

On a particularly hectic day, Hector lent his car to James. Before returning it James called at John Blades's home in Millburn Road. After completing his business, he went outside to discover that the car was missing. The inspector's car had been stolen! The local constabulary recovered the vehicle on a country road behind the Henry Brock Hospital, and in due course the joyrider, Danny, was arrested and taken to court.

Danny was a young man whose over-protective mother had led him to believe that the world owed him a living. Even when he was a child involved in the rough and tumble of play she had been known to raise her tenement window and chastise children for being 'cruel to my Danny', and the boy would strut away like a peacock.

Needless to say, in the home the rod was spared and the spoiled child grew into an arrogant young man. It was that young man who fancied taking the car from Millburn Road, and did just that.

The sheriff who heard the case took this background into account when he sentenced Danny to a short period of imprisonment at

Barlinnie. The punishment might have appeared harsh, but it was to be vindicated by the outcome.

Danny found prison a most unpleasant experience. The strict discipline and spartan conditions had a humbling effect. There was also a threat, albeit imaginary, hanging over him.

He had not known that he was taking the inspector's car and was afraid that after his release he would 'get a good doing'. It was a changed man who told James of his fears in a prison cell. The minister attempted to reassure him, but pointed out that he could not take other people's belongings. He must pay his own way in life – or be prepared to suffer the consequences.

Soon after his release from Barlinnie, Danny moved away from the Vale and James often wondered what had become of him. When James was at Pollok, Danny's mother died. She had requested that Currie should conduct the service at her funeral, so he went back to Millburn. As he walked into the church a woman pushed her way through the mourners, threw her arms around his neck, and gave him a kiss.

'Thank you. You're the man I've got to thank for saving my Danny. He never stops talking about you,' she whispered in his ear.

The woman was Danny's English wife, but it was neither the time nor the place to talk to her, so that evening James returned to tell Peggy that Danny had been 'saved'.

Years later, after speaking at a Burns Supper in England, James was about to leave the hall when Danny came in. He had driven more than a hundred miles to thank James personally for his advice. He had taken it, and now was a millionaire, the income coming from selling cars at the three garages he owned!

James related a similar story, again involving Hector's car and the funeral of a prisoner's mother.

Willie was not a wicked man, but he drank too much and that led to a prison record. Most of his offences involved drink or poaching on Sir Ivor Colquhoun's land, and taking salmon from the River Leven.

He was being held in custody in Barlinnie on such a charge when his mother died. A prison officer escorted him to the funeral. They had to be back at Barlinnie by 5.00 pm, but there was a delay. So that Willie would not get into trouble with the governor, James borrowed his brother-in-law's car and drove the two back to the jail.

On the journey he asked Willie, 'Is it not about time that you found a decent lassie and settled down?'

Willie shook his head ruefully and said, 'Mr Currie, nae decent lassie would have me.'

James reflected later: 'Wasn't that tragic? Imagine going through life with that opinion of yourself. It was terribly sad.'

The minister told Willie that people could change, but he was so saddened by the self-criticism that he feared he was not convincing. When they parted at the gates of the prison the pale-faced man shook James's hand and put on a smile.

Almost thirty years later James went to Dumbarton to open a coffee morning to raise funds for a children's charity. A retired man, his face tanned a rich brown, came over and shook the minister's hand.

'Do you not recognise me?' the man asked.

For once, James's memory failed him.

'I know you all right,' he said, 'but I can't put a name to the face.'

The man gave a clue, 'Do you not remember driving me back to Glasgow?'

The vision of the pale-faced man at Barlinnie came flooding back. The two went to a quiet corner and Willie told his story.

'I did meet a decent lassie and I remembered what you said. I told her the truth about myself and she decided to take a chance on me. Our marriage has been a great success. Booze was the root cause of my problems and she helped me to give it up. I've never had another drink and I've never been back in prison.'

Willie had got his tan from days on the golf course. His evenings were spent at meetings of Alcoholics Anonymous, leading by example and trying to help others with a drink problem.

The details of Danny, the 'man who made a million', would make newspaper headlines, and it brought James a great deal of satisfaction. But he was ecstatic as he related Willie's 'story of sheer triumph'. Not only had a black sheep returned to the fold, he was now working to round up others.

Norman was a quiet, decent man who moved with his parents into the Vale. He did not know anyone there and soon made the wrong kind of friends. One evening they took him to a pub and, because he was not used to alcohol, he got quite drunk. He was afraid to return to his parents' house in that condition, so he went home with one of his new-found friends. During the course of the night, he went to the lavatory. When he came out, the light in the hall had been extinguished. The account of the following events was related at the High Court.

The woman of the house invited Norman into her bedroom. He went in, but some time later attempted to leave. There was a skirmish during which Norman was struck and his spectacles were knocked off. He struck the woman, left the house, and ran home.

In the morning, he remembered that he had left his spectacles at the house so he went back to collect them and to apologise. He was met at the door by a policeman. The woman was dead – killed by a single blow to the throat.

Norman was cautioned and charged with murder. He spent almost six months in custody, during which time he was overwhelmed by guilt and remorse.

When he appeared at the High Court he pleaded guilty. He offered no excuses. He had killed the woman and there could be no justification for that.

The chief superintendent in charge of the case indicated that he wanted to speak, and the Judge heard him. The police officer said that he had charged Norman with murder, but had done so with great regret. He was convinced that the young man had not intended to kill the woman. Her death had been the result of a tragic accident.

James Currie also spoke on behalf of Norman.

The Judge retired briefly to consider the evidence, and then returned to give his verdict. He said that in passing sentence he was taking into account Norman's conscience. If he walked free from the court he would always carry the guilt. Therefore he must pay a price. The Judge sentenced Norman to eighteen months' imprisonment. He had been in custody for almost six months and, with full remission, he was released on parole six months' after the court case.

'That wasn't the end of the story,' James said. 'The Judge had shown great wisdom in recognising Norman's grief and belief that he deserved punishment. In passing a lenient sentence, he hoped that the young man would feel he had paid his debt, but it wasn't so.'

'When Norman came out of prison he was still plagued with guilt. I helped to get him a house away from the area where the death occurred hoping that this would take his mind off it. But it wasn't so.'

'Norman became more and more withdrawn, refusing to allow anyone to get close to him. He couldn't come to terms with his problems and would not allow anyone to help him. Something had to give, but what happened was truly extraordinary.'

Norman's new house was near a railway line. A fence had been broken to allow a short-cut across the track. Although crossing the line was illegal, scores of people did it every day. Norman was crossing when an engine appeared. He tripped, and the engine went over his hand, severing it at the wrist. It was the hand which had struck the fatal blow.

Fate had delivered a punishment that the young man appeared to find acceptable. He began to live again.

A visit to Saughton prison put the final piece in a Millburn jigsaw.

During James's first week at Renton the lead had been stolen from the church hall roof. The new minister suspected it had been done to spite him and a confession in a cell proved this to be true. It also solved the mystery of the twilight figure who roamed the graveyard.

Charlie Craig, clerk to the congregational board, had often reported seeing a man there, always so far away he could not be recognised, but always stopping and staring forlornly towards the church.

We will call the man, haunted by his conscience, Alan. He was, James said, a well-bred man who had been dragged down by unemployment. Alan, who had six children, drank too much, and to get more money for drink he stole. He was an athletic man who owed more than one narrow escape during his nocturnal housebreakings to his fitness. But, he stole too often and was caught. He served a number of terms of imprisonment, and during one of those spells his wife died. When Alan was released, he returned home to look after his family. Considering the strain he must have been under, it was not surprising that on occasions he sought escape in the local pub.

On one night when he had over-indulged, Betty helped him home. Her marriage had broken down and she, too, knew the problems of raising children alone. In the course of time, she and Alan set up home together. Betty was, in Currie's words, 'a decent lassie', one of the major factors required to bring about a reduction in the prison population and a change of course for 'her man'. Alan acquired gainful employment in the building trade and kept on the right side of the law.

One day Betty called at the manse and said she 'wanted the weans done' – baptised. She and Alan had not married. They were not church members and she felt it would not be right for them to go to the kirk. But surely their bairns should not suffer? Would James perform the baptisms at their home?

The request was unique. Certainly, it would be met with disapproval by the Establishment. James's preaching was that the church belongs to the people. The church *is* the people. Here were people making a place for the church in their lives. The official line was clear. How would Currie react?

He said, 'If I refused them, they would see the Church as rejecting them. There was only one thing I could do.'

84

'Can-do' Currie was involved in many conflicts with the 'no-can-do' Establishment. He emerged hurt, but unrepentant.

When he considered Betty's request he asked himself, 'What would Jesus do?' He had no doubt about the answer. He took two elders, to represent the Church, to the home of Alan and Betty. There was some confusion, because Betty's two married daughters were there with their own children but the baptisms, twelve in all, were duly carried out.

Later, James admired an inexpensive print which Betty had hanging on a wall. Then he invited all the members of the family to come to the church and the manse at any time. He left the house, in the certain belief that he had opened doors.

Some months later, Simon, one of Alan's children, became ill and was taken to hospital. James visited the boy there and again met up with Betty. She was going through a particularly worrying time because Alan had been laid off and there was no wage coming into the house. There was also the temptation for him to get money in another way . . .

The evening that Simon was released from hospital there was a power cut in Renton. James got on his bike to ensure that his elderly friends were coping with candles. As he cruised down the hill, the beam from his bicycle lamp lingered for a moment on a silent figure in the shadows. James stopped and the figure came forward. It was Betty. She thrust a parcel wrapped roughly in newspaper under James's arm and said, 'You liked this. You have it. Simon needs boots.' Then she turned on her heel and was gone.

James took the parcel home and unwrapped it, to find the picture he had admired. Simon got his boots, and James kept the picture, 'I didn't want to offend Betty by offering it back.'

James hung the picture in his bedroom. 'She's so soulful. I really love it. It says something to me. I look at her every morning when I wake up.'

The picture was taken with the Curries to Glasgow and then on to Dunlop. It was on James's bedroom wall when he died.

'After he met Betty, Alan never went to prison again – well, only once,' James said.

That was how he came to visit Saughton, and how the truth emerged about the lonely figure at Millburn cemetery. Alan had been unable to get work at home so he had taken a job on a building site at Linlithgow. Without Betty's steadying influence he had got drunk. He told James, 'If I hadn't been drunk I wouldn't have done it. And if I hadn't been drunk I wouldn't have got caught.'

In the cell confessional, Alan went on to say that he had taken the lead off the church hall roof. His guilty conscience had often taken him back to the scene of the crime, which had been committed partly because the new minister had been the focus of so much attention.

Then Alan said: 'If I had known then that you were the man you are I would never have done it. I will spend the rest of my life making it up to you.'

And, James said, he did that. He had suspected that Alan had been responsible for the theft, suspicions strengthened when Alan had given him cash to go towards the cost of the replacement copper. The money, in all probability, had come from the sale of the stolen lead!

Alan was true to his word and, James said, he was proud to call him a friend. On Christmas Eve, Alan accompanied Betty, who by this time was a regular Church attender, to the service at Millburn. About a year later, Betty had a baby. Although the couple still were not married, James persuaded them this child should be baptised in the kirk, and father and mother proudly took their places in front of the congregation.

There is a sad footnote to the story, because one of Alan's sons followed a life of crime. He wrote to James from Barlinnie saying that if the Lord Jesus died for sinners like him then surely he had a right to ask James to put up £32 bail money. Because of the twisted manner of the appeal, it was one of the few occasions when he was reluctant to do so.

'Peggy would go daft if she knew I'd done it,' he said. 'Perhaps you shouldn't mention it in the book.'

'Perhaps you should tell Peggy.'

'Oh, it doesn't matter. She probably found out about it anyway!'

Alan's son is not mentioned as the exception to prove the rule. On the contrary, he simply represents the continuance of the line of, for want of a better word, sinners.

James did not dwell on the reasons why people got into trouble with the law. He concentrated on the good in everybody. 'When you take time to get to know people you find out that really they are ordinary – somebody's father, brother or son. Of course, if they've done wrong they must pay a price. But what does society do for them after exacting its punishment? Surely we have a duty to show some consideration, some kindness?'

Allan Easton laid down the principles: visit the prisons. James Currie made the principle work for the people. And the people, well some of them anyway, responded to him.

'To God be the glory,' James said, and, it is well documented, God works in mysterious ways.

One of James's favourite sayings was, 'You never know the people who will be important in your life.' Such a man was a persistent, unrepentant criminal. The venue for the momentous occasion was a prison cell.

Andy and his brother, Hugh, met only at the gates of Barlinnie. When one was coming out, the other was going in. Their offences took place over a period of about twenty years.

During one visit, Andy confided to James: 'I've been thinkin' it's about time the auld yin started goin' to your church.'

James replied that if Andy did that he would not end up in prison again. Andy changed the subject.

Later that week, the 'auld yin', Andy and Hugh's mother, Mrs F, stopped James in Renton's Main Street.

She said, 'Andy wants me to come to your church. But it's hard. What with the boys and all . . .'

James assured the woman that she would be made very welcome at Millburn, but he appreciated her trepidation so he asked Mrs Blades, the session clerk's wife, if she would go to see Mrs F.

Mrs Blades at first expressed reluctance. She had never gone on such a mission and was concerned that she might say or do something wrong. Then, Mrs F could be lost to the kirk for ever. James asked her just to speak to the lady. Everything would be fine.

That evening, Mrs Blades telephoned the manse. She had just returned from Mrs F's house. She had been given such a lovely welcome there. They'd had tea and a great old blether. Mrs F's fears had been removed and she promised she would come to church on Sunday.

'Oh James,' Mrs Blades said, 'I've never done anything like that for the church. I really feel a Christian now.'

Mrs F went to the church that Sunday and every following Sunday.

'And she brought the folk with her,' James said. 'How she brought the people in.' Some said the kirk wasn't for them but Mrs F told them, 'That's no' what ooor minister says. Our church is for sinners like you an' me.'

Currie was positively beaming. 'Now isn't that tremendous? Is that not just great? Have you heard a better definition?'

A cycle trip to Killearn had brought a grateful mother to the kirk and she had brought along a hundred others. Now a visit to a cell in Barlinnie had won another mother. And she recruited another hundred members for Millburn.

A few years before, the Church of Scotland had deliberated over Millburn's chances of surviving on its own. Amalgamation with a neighbouring parish was considered. In his first days in Renton, James had been told by a fellow minister that 'you can do nothing with the folk of the Vale.'

Currie knew he could do nothing without them. And now the folk of the Vale were doing it for themselves.

CHAPTER ELEVEN

Through a door in faith

Nineteen-fifty-four ended , as it had begun, with the Curries ill on the island of Arran.

The minister had been first to fall foul of a virus. He had collapsed after a rehearsal of the church's pantomime on 22 December and spent the following two days in bed, rising late on Christmas Eve. Despite the fact three local churches – Jamestown, Bonhill North and Bonhill South – had followed Currie's lead and held a Watchnight Service, Millburn enjoyed its biggest attendance.

Three days later, the family was at Drumadoon. James told his diary: 'I must be quite ill for I feel completely helpless and nervously exhausted. The folks at home have been so good and everything is so lovely. I pray God to restore me in body, mind and spirit. Peggy is so good and kind to me. She is helping a lot.'

On 30 December, James went to bed at 7.00 pm. 'I feel so unwell – diarrhoea, palpitations and indigestion.'

He saw in the New Year in bed, reflecting: 'Twenty-two years ago tonight I was lying nearly at death's door with my head split open after going over Balnacoole bridge on my bicycle. Today has not been a pleasant one. I've eaten nothing. Tonight, I feel better and thank God for the year which draws near its close and ask Him for strength to face the one ahead.'

The virus spread through the family and, back at Renton on Saturday 15 January 1955 James Currie prayed for strength to get through the next day's services.

In the morning his sermon, 'The Spirit of the Lord is upon me', was heard with admiration by a Vacancy Committee from St James's Pollok. James did not know the identity of the strangers in the pews or how they would change his life. He noted their presence, but did not give the matter a further thought. The frozen pipes in Millburn Church were uppermost in his mind.

The following Sunday, after preaching that 'Faith without work is dead', he attended a meeting of the kirk session and planned the way forward for Millburn. His priorities were: the deepening of our spiritual life; praying for each other; meetings to discuss spiritual issues; a social club for the 25-40 year olds; and dealing with the lapsed and lapsing.

The next day he received a telephone call from St James's. The committee had decided unanimously that he should be the sole nominee for the collegiate charge at Pollok.

'I told them they were wasting their time,' James said. 'I didn't want to leave Millburn. Why should I? It was going great.'

However, he agreed to go to see the parish and meet the minister there, the Revd Clarence Finlayson. Pollok was a new scheme on the south side of Glasgow. If Currie was looking for a challenge, he had found it. Or rather, it had found him and it was refusing to let go.

After speaking to Clarence Finlayson, James said that he would not change his mind. He was happy at Millburn. Perhaps he did not realise it, or perhaps he was not ready to admit it, but he *had* changed his mind. His diary of that evening records: 'Coming down on the bus I realised how sad I *would* be to leave Millburn. I *will* miss it.' The die was cast.

James Currie had two more things to do before leaving Renton.

The increase in numbers at the kirk and its associated organisations meant that the membership was on the verge of outgrowing the facilities. The small hall, resplendent in its green copper collar, had served its purpose well and, in the early days at Millburn, James would have been happy to have seen its capacity of about one hundred achieved. But that was when there were 237 members on the roll, 'one hundred of them dead, either physically or spiritually.' The church was now a much bigger concern, and its minister had begun to think accordingly. Plans were one thing: realities another. A new, larger hall was certainly desirable, but the cost appeared to put it out of reach.

However, fact, as they say, is stranger than fiction, and the financial facts in the Currie household at that time were an alarming shade of red. The minister could draft grand plans for the kirk, the breadwinner was in debt to the baker.

In an attempt to eliminate the family's overdraft, Peggy got a temporary job as a clerk with Dewrance, an engineering firm in Dumbarton which supplied Babcock. The manse could spare her for a couple of months. The venture was to prove doubly fruitful. The fresh source of finance in the Currie home brought the smile back to the face of the bank manager, and the contact with the company provided the opportunity for Millburn to acquire a new hall.

Dewrance was about to shut up shop and move to England. The prefabricated building which served as its office was surplus to requirements. If Millburn wanted it, and could remove it, the firm was prepared to donate the building to the church.

It was a golden opportunity. The building would easily hold 200 people, exactly what James had been planning. But there were problems to be overcome before the generous offer could be accepted.

The first was the acquisition of a site. There was vacant land between the church and the local chapel. The kirk session agreed to appoint a firm of solicitors to buy it. On 28 January, for the sum of £50, the deal was concluded.

The next hurdle, or so it appeared to James, would be the cost of labour. Building firms did not have the faith of Willie Graham. They would want to see the colour of the money before work began. Once more, God provided, this time in the form of manual labour.

The members of Millburn had a wealth of skills at their fingertips. An appeal for help from the pulpit was met with willingness. On 26 February, the site was cleared. Seven trees were dug up and the holes levelled. Bricklayers, plumbers, electricians and labourers were standing in readiness. The rest would be a dawdle.

With half of his target within his reach, James returned to the manse to start on his second legacy. Although he was tired from working at the site, he planted potatoes – Arran Peaks – in the vegetable bed. That night he telephoned St James's and said he was prepared to accept the post. He told his diary: 'This was an extremely difficult decision to make for I do *not* want to leave Renton. I do *not* want to leave Renton.' The emphasis was clearly marked.

Why had he changed his mind?

The answer is simple. He did what he was told to do.

When he had been teaching at Keil, James Mason persuaded him to apply for three vacant posts at churches. Then Blackburn had accepted him but James Mason told him to reject the offer. Mason was now dead, and so Currie turned to another hero, George Macleod, and told him of the dilemma.

'I said it was a challenge and it excited me but that I didn't want to go,' James said. 'Time and again I told him that I didn't want to go. Millburn was taking off. I loved the people and they loved me.'

George MacLeod listened patiently and then he said: 'James, sometimes a door opens before us. We have not touched that door, but we must go through it in faith.'

James, Peggy and Lord George MacLeod of Fuinary after Charles's christening.

James was not to step through that door until 20 June, and before that there was a lot of work to be done.

He found the next task particularly trying. He wrote a letter to every member of the congregation telling them that he was leaving and thanking them for their suupport and kindness.

Work continued at the site for the hall and 9 April was the day when everything was to come together. The building was dismantled at Dumbarton and taken to Renton by lorry. The gang was ready to assemble it – when disaster struck! There had been an error in the plans and the foundations had been dug, and bricks laid, fifteen inches too far apart.

As the error was discovered, the heavens opened and rain came down in torrents. It would have weakened the resolve of many, but it served only to increase the determination of the kirk's crew.

James told his diary: 'The men gritted their teeth, rallied their strength. Jim Lees and Archie McColl worked in the rain to build another wall. Great stuff! I was proud of them.'

From that day work progressed steadily and without further hitch.

Currie set himself one final task before he left Millburn. In mid-April, when the risk of harsh frost was over, he dug the vegetable gardens at the manse, forked in dung, and planted Arran Peak potatoes. He had done the spadework, the next minister would take care of the parish and the garden. The organic growth was healthy.

In his five years at Millburn, much had been achieved. The manse and its grounds had been renovated; the kirk buildings improved and expanded; and the church had become self-sufficient.

The kirk's roll of 237 with 'one hundred dead either physically or spiritually,' had risen to 1350.

Now Currie had to go through a door in faith . . .

CHAPTER TWELVE

St James, Pollok

If Currie had his reservations over the wisdom of the move, the people at St James's had no doubts that they had chosen wisely.

Clarence Finlayson was equally certain that he had won over the right man to continue the work he had so ably started. Indeed, Finlayson's successes and style of ministry were the major factors which led the Curries leaving the Vale. Finlayson, like many of the men at the kirks in the peripheral estates of Glasgow, was a minister devoted to the parish system. St James's had to serve the needs of *every* household within its boundaries. Its primary purpose was the worship of God and the spreading of His word. James Currie believed this should be done by example: to do unto others as we would have done to ourselves. His role was to help those who needed help – whether they were Church members or not. There were 25 000 people in Pollok. Many of them belonged to other churches, but the remainder were firmly marked down as members of the clan Currie.

James, determined to carry out his work in the community, was eager to get a council house in the parish. However, none was available and wise counsel persuaded the family to view a semi-detached, blonde sandstone house in Dumbreck Road, outside the boundary of St James's but on the number 50 bus route from Pollok. The family looked no further, and 31 Drumbreck Road became their home for fifteen years, and headquarters of a ministry the likes of which may never be seen again. Number thirty-one served as a hostel, social work centre, Red Cross station, and constituency home for the MP for the area who would later become Secretary of State for Scotland.

While the douce residents of Dumbreck and neighbouring Pollok-shields slipped home to their properties after a day in the city, the Currie household, which had been bustling all day, was just starting to get up a head of steam. Its 'members of staff' were many and varied. The finest engines have many components and the big wheel does not turn without the efficient efforts of the small cogs.

The very existence of St James's at Lyoncross Road epitomises the

The Congregational Board of St James.

spirit of Pollok. The church was a 'refugee', a victim of so-called progress. It was formerly Titwood Parish Church in the south side of the city. When the congregations of Titwood and Pollokshields churches merged and moved under the roof of the Pollokshields Kirk, the Titwood building became surplus to requirements. At the same time the City Fathers were busy dispersing the people form the inner-city to the new estates. The population of Pollok was rising steadily and these people wanted a kirk. All that was required was a miracle. It was provided – in the unlikely shape of a coal lorry.

Titwood Church was carefully dismantled and each stone and piece of wood numbered. The lorry undertook the mammoth task of transporting the materials to Lyoncross Road. The lion's share of the work was done by Pollok parishioners and it took three years.

The scriptwriters of Hollywood could not have devised a more ingenious plot. The resurrection of the kirk embodied by the determination of the time. The work was completed in James's early days there, and it was particularly fitting for his beliefs – the people are the Church; and the Church must go to the people.

Pollok provided a bigger stage for Currie's talents, but his role was the same: servant of God, serving the people. To do that he had to get to know them, and that, to James Currie, meant sharing the joys and sorrows of every family. Allan Easton had taught him the way to do that: visit the sick, visit the poor, visit the people in prison, go to see those who need you.

The new firm of Finlayson-Currie and Associates covered the area with a fine-tooth comb. The ministers complemented each other perfectly. Clarence the bachelor with the knowledge of the area; James the family man and eager newcomer. The pair united in spirit, endeavour and visions of the future.

One of the major benefactors of this enthusiastic enterprise was the Ibrox Press. It ran off posters, handbills, leaflets and notices which were distributed to the houses. Long before the ministers knew each parishioner the folk of Pollok knew the ministers. The members of St James's were enlisted in a canvassing campaign which would put a political party's electioneering to shame. Currie cut a dash on the streets on his motor cycle – complete with his bunnet. Heaven's Angel!

The streets were alive with the word, something special is happening, come along and be part of it. One by one they came. They stayed. And they went out to tell others what was on offer. The terms were simple: this is your church, make of it what you will. When they did come, Currie enlisted their talents.

Isabella Williamson was a favourite daughter of Pollok. She sang with Geraldo and Ambrose under the stage name of Anne Haven. When she was to get married to journalist Jack Archer, St James was the place for them. At the time, there was a strike in Rolls-Royce, one of the major employers of Pollok men, and James put both sets of circumstances to good use. The rubble from the reconstruction of the church had not been cleared. From the pulpit, he announced that he wanted volunteers to clear it. 'The men from Rolls-Royce can do it,' he said. The men from Rolls-Royce turned up, and led by James in dungarees and bunnet, they soon had the place neat and tidy. Isabella was delighted. Her wedding photographs would look that bit better. But she did not know that Currie had arranged an unique picture. When the new Mrs Archer came out of St James's she was met by a guard of honour – the workmen with crossed shovels!

The photograph appeared in the daily newspapers. There was something special happening at Pollok. The name of the kirk was on everyone's lips. A kirk where there was laughter and something different happening. The recipe was right, and at its peak St James's had 3000 members and a further 7000 were regular attenders.

I asked the Church of Scotland how many kirks today have a membership of 3000. The answer is none. St James's role today is around 500.

So how was the phenomenon of Pollok achieved?

Time and again I asked James Currie this question. He said he could not answer it. He said simply, 'It was God's will.'

Amen. But let us take a look at the work of His Servant.

The Pollok days were the pinnacle of Currie's illustrious career. He scaled it with the assistance of many, many people, but the golden days of St James's are inextricably intertwined with the name of James Currie. Let us go back to 31 Dumbreck Road to examine the man beneath the clerical robes. What was his outlook?

'James was driven by his work,' says Peggy. 'It's the only way to describe it. His work was everything. He was an obsessive – couldn't do anything in moderation. And he would end up exhausting himself and everyone around him.'

The minister was at the beck and call of his flock. That was the first and last rule in the Currie household and it left precious little time for the duties and pleasures of the husband, father and friend. He jumped when the parish called, and he demanded that his family and friends do likewise when he needed them. And that was often. If they failed him, or if he *felt* they failed him, the man whose stock in trade was understanding, compassion and forgiveness would go into a huff. Sometimes for a week. Peggy took the brunt of it, but faithful friends were also 'punished'.

Laura Kennedy, a nursing sister at Stobhill Hospital at the time, was a stalwart in Dumbreck Road. She would be nannie to the boys, cook, bottle-washer, driver, speaker at meetings in place of James – a loving and devoted friend. She was next in line to receive the wrath of the minister. James would exact retribution if he felt let down.

Phyllis Wright, now Mrs McLeod, was a schoolgirl with ambitions of becoming a secretary. One day she admired a typewriter in the vestry. In the blinking of an eye, James 'engaged' her as unpaid, over-worked personal secretary. After school the girl would take down in shorthand dozens of the minister's letters then type them. In between, she helped tend to the constant flow of visitors to the manse. The girl's loyalty and efficiency was frequently rewarded with the sharp edge of Currie's tongue.

'He didn't mean it,' said Phyllis, who went on to become personal secretary of a busy procurator-fiscal. 'It was just Mr Currie's way when he was really tired. We all knew it – and he was so sorry and so nice afterwards.'

James Currie gave so much of himself to his parish that often he had nothing left for those closest to him. The more he gave the more he was obliged to give. And then he cracked. At home. Where his weaknesses were understood. Where they would be hidden. And where he would be cossetted, coaxed, cajoled and rejuvenated to return to the streets afresh . . . until the next time.

His huffs were often planned. When all else proved fruitless, when persuasion and 'blackmail' failed to win his way, he would sulk. He knew Peggy and the others could not bear to see him this way. They would yield, eventually, to keep the peace.

Peggy said: 'James was a complex man. I loved him dearly and sometimes it was just as well for he could be exasperating – terribly difficult to live with.'

The nervous breakdown which overwhelmed him in West Pilton in 1947 frequently threatened to resurface. It was contained, restricted to depressions. And while he brooded in the manse the telephone would call him to duty. He would don a face with his overcoat and go to help the caller. He gave comfort to others while he was in despair.

Another enigma in the Currie make-up was the tightrope he trod between egotism and shyness. He was an accomplished performer, a 'natural' who held an audience spellbound. But he was bashful, self-critical and hypersensitive. He needed shoring up. Again, only those close to him could do this, and it called for a delicate balance of critical appraisal and admiration. He loathed congratulations which were not sincere. 'Being damned with faint praise', was how he put it.

James's father died during the Pollok days and the tenancy of Drumadoon died with him. James, the eldest son, would have had first claim to it had he been an Arran farmer, but, of course, he was a minister on the mainland. There was great speculation on the island over who would move into Drumadoon. But Currie had other ideas. Tobago's legacy was not to be squandered. He argued his case to take over the tenancy. He would personally supervise the well-being of the farm and put in a manager. Peggy had a degree in agriculture and had worked Drumadoon since she was a girl. No one knew the place better. And he had three strapping boys growing up. They would help, and in course one of them would take up the reins. The decision to allow the minister to take over the tenancy of the farm caused consternation and not a little anger on Arran.

The problems were obvious. Two generations of the Currie family had sweated full-time to eke a living out of the farm. Now, in the midst of a demanding role in a thriving parish, James had taken on the burden of responsibility in his 'spare time'. There can be no question that his heart ruled his head. If he had considered the situation dispassionately for one minute he would have had to admit that his wishes were, at best, impractical. For a start, he had no spare time. His attitude to how he must serve the people often left him exhausted. He would not compromise his role as a parish minister. But he could not be swayed. Indeed, he was not willing to limit his position to that of tenant of Drumadoon. He wanted to buy it, and, after proving that he could cope with the difficulties of being a long-distance farmer, that is what he did. Or, to be more accurate, he took out a whacking great mortgage on the place.

Currie, the farmer, took great satisfaction from breaking new ground. Fields at Drumadoon were dear to his heart because he had 'created' them – hacked out boulder and bracken root, ploughed in seaweed as fertiliser, and won a green acre from infertile scrubland. That done, he was happy to leave its maintenance to others.

The minister tried to work to a similar pattern. He was a man for the black sheep. While the faithful flock of St James's was never deprived, the sinners in the parish received most of his attention. And the sinners came from the unlikeliest of places. There were those in the criminal fraternity, errant husbands and wives, and people whose lives were in turmoil. But the biggest burden on the entire Currie household was a woman holding a respectable job, who was, on the surface, a pillar of the kirk.

James Currie held a 'vestry night' every Wednesday. It was an open forum where individuals could discuss kirk matters, offer names of people in the parish who needed assistance, or seek help and advice for their personal problems. James knew that it took courage for folk to admit that they needed help. They would breeze in and talk about anything and everything except the one matter they really wanted to discuss.

'When folk come to see you the last thing people say is the most important,' James said. 'That's the real reason why they come along. That's a good thing for any minister, or anyone else in our type of profession, to remember.'

So it was with this particular woman, who shall be called Mary. As a member of the congregation who took an active part in the running of the church, she was often at the vestry night meetings, always on the periphery. James felt that she wanted to talk about something, and one night after all the visitors had left, he engaged Mary in conversation.

It transpired that she was a secret drinker who had never found the courage to accept that she was an alcoholic. She would drink before going to work, sneak out for what appeared to be a social drink at lunch time, then have some more before going home with a bottle hidden in her handbag. Only the members of her immediate family knew the depths of her dependence on alcohol, and, in shame, they covered it up. James had worked with problem-drinkers before and laid great store in the fellowship of Alcoholics Anonymous, but the woman refused to go to their meetings. As she became more dependent on drink, so her dependence on the minister increased. He would collect her from various parts of the city at all hours of the day and night. If he was not available, Peggy or Laura Kennedy or some other trusted member of No 31 would fill in.

Early one morning Mary telephoned the manse. She was in town. Could James collect her and drive her home. He pulled an overcoat on top of his pyjamas and set out for her. Mary was terribly drunk, ashamed, and did not want the neighbours to see her in that condition. As they drove back, they were stopped by a police patrol car. Sensing something was wrong, the officers asked the driver to get out of his car. The minister's attire took a bit of explaining.

Inevitably, Mary became known to the police. James spoke to the duty officers in the surrounding divisions, leaving word that if Mary was picked up by any policeman he should be contacted. The result of this was that the telephone in the manse would ring and someone had to be despatched to a police office or hospital to collect her. The story does not have a happy ending. Mary never overcame her dependence on alcohol and died in tragic circumstances.

Another frequent figure at the manse was a local woman who had fallen on hard times and resorted to the oldest profession – prostitution. One night James found her, forlorn and bedraggled, wandering the streets. he took her home with him, where Peggy prescribed hot soup and listened to the sorry story until the early hours. By that time the woman was too late and too tired to go anywhere, so she spent the night on the Curries' bed-settee. The boys, who were not unaccustomed to unusual visitors, were curious about the brassy breakfast guest. Their mother explained later that she was a lady who needed help.

But the visit was not an isolated incident. Later that month the woman telephoned No 31. She had been thrown out of her house. Could she spend the night at the manse? James collected her in his car and this time he had a long conversation with her. Surely she realised this was no way to live? What could he do to help her sort out her life? The woman assured him that she had seen the error of her ways and would try her best to correct them.

They were empty words, and, after several other nocturnal conversations, Peggy realised it. She spoke to her husband and asked him to stop bringing the woman to the manse. James was hurt and angry, so he sulked. Peggy tried to explain that it was not fair to the boys. James refused to listen. The woman needed help. That was obvious. She could turn to no one else so she came to the servant of God. Was he to desert her too?

The simplicity of his argument, and proven power of his huffs, won his case. The telephone calls, and visits at all hours of the day and night continued. Then Peggy discovered the woman had venereal disease.

'That was it,' she said. 'I refused point-blank to allow her over the doorstep. James tried to talk me out of it but I refused to budge. But that's the way he was. He was a *good* man. I see now what he was trying to do. I just wish he could have explained it at the time. But I'm not sure that he really knew. If someone, anyone, needed help then James believed it was his duty to do what he could. And that meant it was his family's duty too. I felt there were limits to what we could do, but James never countenanced limitations.'

This fundamental disagreement was at the root of most of the quarrels in the home. James said that his wife did not 'suffer fools gladly', while he thought that everyone deserved a chance – and another chance . . . Peggy believed that there came a time when their kindness was abused, when some folk looked on James as a 'soft touch', and when the happiness and welfare of her own family was the priority.

Who was right? The minister who put the welfare of the people of his parish above all else or the mother protecting her sons?

It is tempting to say that both were correct. But No 31 did not run on theory. This frequent argument was a battle of wills invariably won by the mothering instinct. James continued to try to help the prostitute and others like her, but was debarred from bringing them to the manse. Each battle was fought individually, the passions and logic the same, and the outcome a bitter quarrel, a Currie huff, until Peggy gave some ground and coaxed him out of it.

One chapter of events could have had tragic repercussions for the Currie family. The minister was told of a feud in which one man, let us call him Ralph, had sworn that he would kill his brother-in-law. James visited the homes, asking if he could help. Surely nothing could be so serious? Perhaps he could act as go-between, a mediator, and heal the rift? All indications were that Ralph was unstable and capable of carrying out his threat, so James went to see him last. He discussed the problem with the man. After a while, Ralph appeared to calm down. He would not kill his brother-in-law, but he would not forgive him. Progress, crisis over, James thought, he was mistaken.

Ralph had a fearsome temper which flared frequently. The telephone at the manse would ring with news that he 'was going to do it this time'. Relatives would call James to tell him that Ralph had a knife, a hatchet, or some other lethal weapon. The minister would bring the disturbed man to No 31 to try to soothe him and defuse the situation. Unknown to Peggy, Ralph was telling James that he had serious financial worries. James was giving him money.

One day Ralph called at the manse demanding cash. James was visiting patients in the Southern General Hospital and Peggy was out shopping. The three Currie boys were alone in the manse. Young James, who had just come home from High School, answered the knock on the door. He told Ralph he had no money and refused to allow him into the house. The man's temper exploded, and he produced a knife.

'You'll be sorry,' he shouted, 'I'm going to kill your father. You tell him. I'll kill him.'

Iain, who was only nine, overheard the threat and saw the knife. He burst into tears and ran to fetch Charles. By the time Charles had calmed down his younger brother and raced to the door there was no sign of Ralph or James. Charles ran round the corner and found James telling the man in no uncertain terms not to return to the manse.

'If you do, you'll have me to answer to. And my brother as well.'

As Charles arrived, Ralph saw that the protective sons meant what they said. He did not return to No 31, but continued to seek out the minister until he left the parish.

Several years later the man became one of Scotland's most notorious multiple killers and is now in the State Hospital, Carstairs.

James Currie, was a well-known face in the courts of Glasgow. The presbytery put forward ministers, on a rota basis, to open the High Court with prayer. James made it a point on these occasions, where possible, to speak to the judges, lawyers, court officials and policemen.

He saw it as part of his job to appear in court to speak on behalf of parishioners facing charges, and he had no intention of doing so as a stranger. He carried out his duty well, and was respected by both the establishment and the 'streetwise'.

A courtroom might appear an unlikely recruiting ground for the Kirk, but Currie believed that offering support at such traumatic times was essential. This did not mean being economical with the truth or offering character references seen through rose-coloured spectacles. 'It was enough just to *be* there,' he said.

It offered contact, an opportunity for honesty and trust not only with the accused but with the close friends and relatives. These opportunities were never wasted. James recorded every court appearance in his diary, noting names of accused, witnesses and officials he had met. He would go over his notes from time to time, matching faces with the names and imprinting them on his 'photographic memory'. Then he would go out of his way to meet the folk.

He continued to carry out Allan Easton's advice and visit the prisons. On one occasion, the governor of Barlinnie accompanied him through the passageways to see a Pollok man who had been sent away for a long time. James knew the names of many of the prison officers, and wished them good morning. They replied: 'Good morning, Mr Currie,' and offered a respectful 'Sir' to the governor. However one officer, perhaps flustered when his superior arrived unannounced, said: 'Good morning, Mr Currie and er . . . em.'

'Well,' the governor chuckled, 'I'd heard it said but now I know it's true. You're better known in here than me.'

'He was joking,' James said. 'But I was chuffed. That was really taking the Church to the people, and people who needed it. And they listened to me. Mind you, I had a captive audience!'

James kept a list of people who were being released from prison and made a point of visiting them as soon as they got home.

'That's when they're most vulnerable. Perhaps they're ashamed, or some may be boastful, but they're all impressionable. Particularly young folk. Some of them may have been imprisoned, and rightly, but without doing anything really bad. They might well have fallen into bad company inside prison. It's important to show that folk still care for them and they can mend their ways.'

Many of these youths came from Peggy's youth club. Frequently, when happy stories emerged from the hall at Barnbeth, it was James's youth club. But even Currie the optimist, the man who looked back on 'glorious, golden days', recognised that the club saw its share of troubles. And its existence was often in jeopardy.

Amenities in the large housing estate were few and far between, and there was the grand total of nothing for young folk. Even getting permission to use corporation playing fields was a minefield of red tape and bureaucracy. James began the club in the early 1960s to offer the youth of Pollok a place to go off the streets. It was the era of gangs. The Govan Team, The Bundy Boys. And the Pollok Crew. There was territorial warfare, with serious injury inflicted by fearsome weapons. At the club they could play table tennis, talk, arrange their own dances. James bought a second-hand juke box, which proved a great attraction. But the running of the club fell to Peggy and her trusty sidekick Laura. Their methods and organisation were unconventional, to say the least, but they prevented many a battle, were influential in many a young life, over their thirteen-year 'reign'.

Life held nothing to surprise Peggy Currie or Laura Kennedy. If the parish minister's wife and casualty nursing sister had not seen it they had heard about it. They could not be shocked. But the 'hard men' of Pollok could be, and they were, when they tried to take on this partnership.

'Right from the start we stood no nonsense,' Peggy said. 'If we'd shown any signs of weakness we would have been doomed. They'd have run over the top of us. So we appeared stentorian harridans. It worked, and the boys respected us for it.'

The Cave, as the club became known, had three rules which had to be obeyed.

No fighting.

No vandalism.

No weapons.

Those entering The Cave left their 'tools' in a cupboard at the door. Knives, hatchets, batons and knuckledusters were safely deposited in the armoury at the Kirk and the youths 'and the girls – some of them were just as bad', collected them on the way out. These processes were supervised by the gang leaders. Peggy and Laura deliberately distanced themselves, for obvious reasons.

Laura said, 'I know many folks will frown on this, but if boys from the gangs came to the club were we supposed to turn them away? After all, they were the lads who most needed a place to go. They would have had every right to have felt alienated if we had refused to let them in. We took them off the streets, away from trouble for a while, and gave them something to do.'

How was discipline maintained and punishment administered.

Long before 'Arfur' Daley of television fame became a folk hero, Peggy and Laura had their minders – the gang leaders – the hard men feared and obeyed by the others. Admittedly, there were terms of indiscipline when these unlikely custodians of the law were themselves brought to justice for their own misdemeanours on the streets and locked away in one of Her Majesty's institutions. However even 'inside' they learned of any troubles and instructed their lieutenants to restore order at The Cave.

'Some of the boys – the gang leaders – really looked after us,' Laura said. 'If they'd been in prison or borstal we'd butter them up when they came out. "Oh Jimmy, I'm so glad you're back. I couldn't do anything with his lot when you were away. Now don't you let me down again." And he'd say, "Aye, alright then, just tell me who's been giving you trouble and I'll sort them out." And he did.'

'They weren't bad boys – I'm not saying they were angels, far from it – but they weren't bad.'

The woman reminisced, bemoaning the episodes they had missed of 'Dr Finlay's Casebook' to open The Cave. There are stories of fracas involving the police, smashed 'lavvies', heated discussions with the kirk session threatening to close the club with Peggy and Laura in 'the boy's corner'; and memories of the boys forming a protective guard to get the women out of the area when rival gangs descended.

This was how the parish system was run in Pollok. It meant taking the Church to the people – and the 'boys' were the people just as much as the old folk in homes or those who attended the kirk's jumble sales. The women did not look back on these times as 'golden days'.

Peggy said, 'We were mad. When you think back on it we were mad. The police would be waiting outside the club at closing time. Or they would try to come in – I wouldn't let them. Outside. You can speak to them outside. In here they're mine.'

She raised her arm pointing firmly to the door of the manse in Dunlop. It was not difficult to imagine a policeman in Pollok obeying the instruction.

Then Peggy told of one of the few times she had cried in church. She is not a woman to weep in pubic – 'it's so undignified' – but one of her 'boys' brought tears to her eyes. He was remembered as a 'scruffy wee boy, quite smelly and insignificant.' He had married and moved out of the parish. When his first child was born he returned to ask if James would baptise the infant. Currie, of course, was delighted and the date was set. However, when that Sunday came along the young man's wife was ill in bed with 'flu. Nevertheless, he boarded the bus with his first-born and stood proudly in St James's Church.

'It sounds nothing special,' Peggy said. 'But I was so proud of that boy. Before I knew it the tears were dripping off my cheeks. Marriage was the making of that lad. He's a church elder today.' Ventures like The Caves were bringing people towards the Church. As in Renton, these people brought others who brought others. The Church belonged to the people and now they were beginning to belong to it.

Many folk were in the category of 'undecided', and one classic piece of marketing was about to bring them into the Currie camp. But it almost never happened. In September 1967, James was invited to be a judge at STV's Miss Scotland competition. In those days such events were regarded as beauty contests with few voices raised in complaint about the so-called 'female cattle show'. However, James was dubious over the wisdom of appearing. Perhaps it was not the place for a man of the cloth to be.

Peggy had no doubts. 'You must go where the people go. You have to meet them on their ground,' she told him.

On the day of the competition James rose at 8.00 am after four hours' sleep. He had a hectic schedule – hospital visits, meetings with church organisations, and people to see in their homes. After lunch, he spoke at Laurel Bank school's scripture union and then changed into his robes to conduct three weddings. Everything was going smoothly until there was an accident in the Clyde tunnel. The parents of the bride of the 5.00 pm wedding at St James's were stuck in traffic. James had to *ad lib* for twenty minutes until they arrived. After that, there was no time for dinner. James had promised to show his slides of the Holy Land in Tweedsmuir, Peeblesshire. He began the meeting but had to leave Peggy and Laura in charge and race back to the Cowcaddens studio as the show was going on the air. Camilla Smith, Miss Troon, was duly elected winner and Currie's face covered the front page of the newspapers giving her a kiss. He certainly was meeting the people. One way or another his face was in every livingroom in Scotland.

'It was the best thing I ever did,' he said. 'You've no idea the amount of interest it raised. Men were stopping me in the streets to say I had "nae taste", because Camilla's make-up didn't show her to best advantage on television. But the men who used to avoid me were crossing the street to talk to me. You think she's bad? I asked them. Come along to church and see my wife!'

Currie became a 'regular' on television, not just on late night religious slots but on current affairs programmes where his outspoken views often flew in the face of the establishment. He made himself, and therefore St James's Pollok, known. But it proved to be a curse as well as a blessing.

The telephone in No 31 rang in the early hours one morning and a woman said she had seen James on television. He had spoken about brotherhood and equality. Could he give her £600?

Currie's style had always raised eyebrows in the Kirk's hierarchy, but now he was receiving reminders of Church policy and official letters of rebuke. Such chastisements are not uncommon, but James took them to heart and exacerbated the situations by entering into lengthy and occasionally heated correspondence. His watchword on each occasion was: have I done what Christ would have done? When he answered the question in the affirmative, he defended his actions stoutly.

He had one recurring argument with the establishment. His willingness to baptise children born to Roman Catholics. Currie the 'bluenose, the bigot' would not yield on this. If people came to him, to his church, and he believed them to be genuine he would conduct the christenings.

Another point of contention with authority was when he conducted ceremonies 'outwith his territory'. Each minister and each kirk has its own boundaries. It is frowned upon to stray into another parish. However Currie's high profile, and the spread of knowledge that he was willing to defy this convention brought an increasing number of requests to conduct weddings, funerals and christenings.

Many ministers firmly believe that all people are encouraged to join the Church. Those who exercise this right are entitled to make full use of their kirk and minister. Others who choose not to, need not expect the Church to be at their beck and call. There is no Kirk dogma on this. Ministers are left to decide by their own beliefs and consciences.

Currie was firmly opposed to the view that the Church was a club, or a limited company, which catered only for the needs of its members or shareholders. He crossed swords frequently with members of the old school, arguing that their blinkered view was unchristian.

'We're supposed to open the doors of the Church not slam them in people's faces,' James said. 'What should I have done when people asked me to conduct a funeral in Inverness? Say no? Who would that have helped? Certainly not the mourning family or the Church.'

He never said 'No'. If he had a prior engagement he would do his best to contact a similar thinking minister to conduct the service. This too, led to letters of complaint and allegations of the 'Currie Clan'.

What did James Currie gain from these affairs. Money, kudos, glory from thumbing his nose at authority?

Let us first take a brief look at his financial affairs. James Currie could not tell me how much he was paid at West Pilton, Renton, Pollok or Dunlop. 'I never asked what the stipend was. It's not a job you do for money.' He did know that when he moved to Pollok he was out of pocket. The stipend was much the same, but he had a travel allowance at Renton. So moving to Glasgow meant belts had to be tightened further.

Bridegrooms in Scotland usually give the minister a 'gift'. It is not required, because conducting a wedding is the most pleasant part of a minister's duties, but it is one of the traditions which flourishes in the allegedly tight-fisted race. Few kirks have full-time, paid organists, so when a minister arranges for one to play at a service he feels obliged to meet travelling expenses. From the beginning of his ministry, James Currie gave a Bible to every couple he married. This was his gift, his reminder that the vows had been taken before God.

'I know some folk say that James "made a fortune out of weddings". I refer them to our bank manager. We were in the red until I took a full-time job teaching,' Peggy said.

Kudos? The lifeblood of leaders and egotists. The highest honour in the Church of Scotland is to be elected Moderator of the General Assembly. Any young minister with ambitions of achieving this goal would do well to study Currie's personal style – and avoid emulation at all costs. Each organisation has a grudging respect and admiration for the angry young man. The older, experienced campaigner who kicks at the traces is a trouble-maker. James Currie knew the rules and regulations. He knew how to 'play the game'. But he knew he could not live with his conscience if he did.

He was not an ambitious man. He was too shy, too insecure to be so. But he was a devout believer in the parish system, and was roused to anger at what he considered to be its demise. He well knew that the way to change the direction was to take a hold of the reins, but to do that he would have to 'play the game'.

Was he frustrated that he never attained higher office?

'I never looked for that kind of thing,' he said.

When pressed, he admitted that he would have 'served if called upon to do so'.

Was he disappointed that he did not get the call.

'Let's just say this. I climbed to the top of the heap at every stage. At primary school, at Keil, University and Trinity College. But I never wanted to be Moderator. I'd have been hopeless anyway.'

So did he enjoy defying authority?

As stated previously, his views on life and its injustices were formed at an early age and did not alter. At first glance this appears surprising, particularly for a man who met so many people from all walks of life and was widely read. However on closer examination, it is what should be expected because the character of James Currie, 'The Minister' from the playground, was cast early. The boy who cried when a teacher called him by his surname grew into the youth who ate his sandwiches in the lavatory and became the man who needed bolstering all his life. Part of James Currie was sheepish – the part that his father saw when he forced the boy into Ogham Cave – but the man recognised this and knew that he had to overcome it. When confrontation was inevitable, when he heard the cock crowing three times, he first fought his own weakness and then set out to fight his fight. His diaries record little of the anger, but much of the pain of battle. He did not see himself as a natural leader, but felt morally-bound to speak out when no one else would. In many contests the odds were stacked against him and he knew the result was inevitable. That did not stop him from fighting. That did not stop him from feeling hurt and inadequate when he lost.

In one David and Goliath contest he took on Billy Graham. The evangelist had become a folk hero in the United States and was packing halls all over Britain with his spectacular rallies. Thousands of people were going forward 'to be saved'. There was laughter, happiness, a wind of change which might be thought to have the blessing of Currie, the master of the media. But he was vehemently opposed to the 'swashbuckling style and promises of living happily ever after'.

He contained his anger until Billy Graham's rally at Glasgow's Kelvin Hall. One teenage girl, a regular attender at St James's, wrote and told James that she had attended the rally and had 'been saved'. Currie wrote to the newspapers and spoke on television in opposition to the 'mass hysteria which Billy Graham whipped up'.

James said, 'It's easy to promise sweetness and light. But being a Christian is not about that. Christ never promised an easy life. He said, "lift up your cross and follow me". But people were going forward, swept away in the euphoria, as if they'd won the pools, thinking all their worries were over. What happens when they wake up and find they still have all of their problems? How do they feel then? They feel let down, betrayed, and they're further away from the Church than ever.

109

'And what about the people who'd "been saved and born again". Many of them were Christians, good folk already attended church. But they were encouraged to step forward to boost their sales figures. Billy Graham did more harm than good.'

Similar criticisms have been laid at Currie's door. Where are the 3000 members of St James's today?

'They're spread throughout churches all over Scotland. But that's not the question you should be asking. You should be asking why people don't go to church today.'

Why don't they?

'Because they think they don't want to. Because the Kirk has become so wrapped up in itself, in its rules and dogma, that it's forgotten what it's for. The Church is for the people. We should be asking what can we do for them, not what can they do for us?'

The words of a Moderator? Perhaps. Those of an aspiring Moderator? Definitely not.

If James Currie did not see himself as a leader of men he was certainly seen as one, and one who led from the front. Whether it was clad in dungarees removing rubble from the kirk gardens or spending an entire evening visiting people in hospital wards, he led by example. He would not ask anyone to tackle anything he would not do himself.

He loved to laugh, but perhaps even more, he loved to make others laugh. He was a marvellous story-teller, and many of the 'experiences' he related were completely credible until he delivered the punchline.

One of his favourites was about a christening in St James's, where it was not uncommon for sixty proud parents to be gathered with their offspring. When James asked one young father the name he had chosen for his daughter the man replied, 'Spindona'.

There is nothing new under the sun, so when Currie held this particular child at the font he duly said: 'I christen thee Spindona'.

'What?' the father interjected. 'Her name's Margaret. See – I wrote it on this label.' He pointed to a piece of paper pinned on to the girl's christening robe.

Currie (in a low voice): 'But I asked you the name and you said Spindona.'

'Aye,' the father said. 'You asked me and I told you it's pinned on her.'

The story is told, liberally interspersed with laughter, in a broad accent.

'And that's why there's a wee girl somewhere called Spindona.'

It's a good story (probably apocryphal), but the telling is better.

Nineteen proud mothers and only one minister! A group christening at St James.

You laugh at the tale, then you laugh with the teller. Then he laughs again and you can't help but join him. Even with an audience of one, Currie timed the punchline, milked the story, then he was off on to another one. The performer had raised a laugh. He wanted more.

'It's like last week when I visited the Victoria Infirmary. I was early, just after breakfast, but a young priest was already half-way down the ward. After about half an hour he came to me and said, "Goodness, there's a lot of Catholics in this week".'

The laughter overtakes him. He has told the story a hundred times but he can't stop himself chuckling. I laugh at him laughing.

'And I said to him well actually, most of these folk are Protestant.' 'You're wrong,' he replied, showing me a list at the ward sister's desk. 'See,' he said, pointing to the names, 'nineteen RCs and only five Ps.'

More laughter.

'And I said to him it's your first time here, isn't it? That's the breakfast list – rice crispies and porridge!'

And he goes on. 'I heard a great one yesterday. From a wee five-year-old . . . hold on, wait till I get it right.'

111

He empties the pockets of his robes. A large forearm brushes clear a space at the kitchen table, already a mass of newspapers, letters, scraps of paper. The space rapidly becomes filled with two pieces of string; a half-eaten packet of mints; innumerable scraps of paper, one of which was last Sunday's sermon.

'Where is it now? I wonder where Peggy put it. I can't leave anything down in this place.'

'This place', and the livingroom, and every other room for that matter, is swallowed up by his filing system. His study, a generous room, seems to shrink with the mass of books, letters and documents which spill out of bookcases and cupboards. The walls and tops of furniture creak with souvenirs. There is a route to the desk through the piles of books on the floor, if you take large strides and have the technique of a high-hurdler. Peggy is banned from the study. Peggy's friends, and anyone else who 'puts things in other places', dare not attempt to set foot in the study. Currie knows when it is time to tidy the study. That time is when even he cannot clear the hurdles.

He cannot find the slip of paper which is the key to the five-year-old's joke, but he tells the tale anyway. 'That's not right,' he says. 'It's better than that. But I'll work on it.'

He would work on it when he had the time. When he had only two other things to do. James Currie devoured work. It was like a god to him. He could not simply do one thing. He did not appear relaxed unless all round him was in confusion.

When I spoke to him I set up a microphone and tape recorder. He talked to it easily, and the system meant that I did not have to write down every word but could concentrate on noting points which should be explained more fully. One thing at a time is a challenge to me.

James would talk happily, describing incidents and events in detail. A biscuit barrel propped up *The Glasgow Herald*, and, as he turned the pages in mid-sentence, he would take the opportunity to capture another Kitkat. His right hand, as if by its own volition, would be answering letters.

His telephone must have been made of asbestos. Five minutes is a long time between telephone calls in Currie's manse. Ring ring. Tape off, Phone lifted. Conversation engaged. Right hand writing. Left hand turning pages of the newspaper.

One thing at a time is enough for me. Often I had to play back the tape to find out what James had said. The thing I had been doing was watching him. And that tired me. However listening to the tapes was never time-consuming. On one visit to the manse, when there was

112

only me, James, and the telephone for five hours, the tape-recorded interview lasted thirteen minutes. Much of the time is accompanied by the rustling of chocolate biscuit papers, the scraping of butter on toast and the clink of teacups. James would return from his telephone conversation and pick up the story exactly where he had left off.

The 'thirteen-minute marathon' tape concludes with, 'Here, Billy Boy, just write some of these Christmas cards while we blether. Pass me that marmalade, please. Is there another cup of tea in the teapot?'

The most productive interviews are conducted over the whine of my car engine. The noise from the engine is imperceptible because the heater fan is on full blast. Currie, who is some place under the layers of clothing and massive coat, does not like the cold. It is so hot the wing mirrors are steamed up. The heater fan is inaudible for five minutes while he shaves with his battery razor. This is the only way to get him alone. My dashboard is melting. But it is worth it. He is describing Alex Smith and the consecration of the cemetery at Alexandria. His recall is remarkable . . . 'a dark black night, and Alex's wee dog, a Heinz, fifty-seven varieties, with one ear folded over which made it look as if it was always smiling . . .' The descriptions are vivid; the stories extraordinary. Honestly, I could write a book . . .

My interviews and conversations with James Currie were conducted over his last years, while he was at Dunlop, when he was under doctor's orders to slow down. But he had only one pace – flat out. He devoured work. If it was a god to him, he worshipped it faithfully to the end. His personal popularity never diminished, and he was in great demand as a speaker at all sorts of functions. Even after he had to admit that his health had deteriorated, he could not decline an invitation. His parishioners never suffered from lack of attention. They received at least eight hours of Currie's day, as advocated by the Iona Community. However this very guideline led to Currie being thrown out of the Community in his Pollok days.

The parting was painless because the love had faded and the two had become estranged. An edict had been sent out that each minister should complete and return to the Community a detailed description of how they had spent their eight-hour day. This Currie steadfastly refused to do, arguing that he was too busy doing to write about what kept him busy. Ironically, while Pollok was being proclaimed living proof of the benefits of the Community's principles, its discipline was cast out.

'It saddened me,' James said. 'Not because I had been turfed out – I invited that – but because the Community had become a bit quaint. It had become too wrapped up in its own existence and forgotten its true purpose.'

There can be no doubt that Currie earned his corn in Pollok. The climbing roll at St James was testament to that, and one of the major reasons for this was the widespread appeal of the church's organisations. The young folk flocked to Sunday School, Bible Class, Youth Fellowship and The Cave. There were guilds for the women, men's councils, industrial groups, prayer meetings, and intercessary services where folk prayed for the sick by name. James ensured that there were regular speakers at the functions – ministers, people in the news, dignatories from abroad. These people came to St James's, and in return Currie went to talk at their own organisations. His diaries are crammed with appointments, sometimes three in a day, as he repayed his obligations.

In the mid 1960s he got the opportunity to visit the Holy Land. The experience thrilled and excited him, and opened two new avenues of activity. He became an unofficial courier taking parties on guided tours of the Holy Land, and made contact with *The Sunday Post*, and became a regular contributor to its widely-read columns. The minister with the human touch, the man who made people laugh and comforted them when they cried, was like a godsend to the newspaper. But they met under the most inauspicious of circumstances.

On his first visit to the Holy Land Currie returned with a bottle of water from the River Jordan. He used this to baptise children in St James's. He told an elder about the special significance of the ceremony, completely ignorant of the furore it would cause. The elder told another church officer who told a friend and the story grew like 'Topsy'. Later that week the father of one of the children who had been baptised got into an argument with a Roman Catholic in a pub. One word led to another, and the contretemps ended with the Catholic saying that the man in St James's was really 'one of our's. He baptised weans with Holy Water.'

The man was so incensed by this that the telephoned *The Sunday Post* complaining that a Kirk minister had no right to do such a thing. A reporter was duly despatched to check the veracity of the story. When the allegations were put to Currie he realised the implications of his actions and that naiveté was a poor excuse for the storm which could be whipped up. Naturally, he could not lie about the facts, but . . . there was another way. If there is one thing a reporter likes better than a story it's a better story. Currie laid one in his lap. It had all the ingredients of a *Sunday Post* classic.

A Glasgow woman had contacted him before his visit to the Holy Land. Her son had been killed in the Palestine campaign during the Second World War. His body lay somewhere in a humble war grave. She had never been well enough to try to find it; could not even send a wreathe. But there was one way she could get peace of mind . . . She gave James a sprig of white heather and asked him to plant it at the grave. Her son was a proud Scot. Part of his native land would be with him for ever.

At that time, as it is today, the Middle East was a simmering cauldron of hatred with frequent eruptions of violence. The minister made enquiries during his visit to the Holy Land and was told that the young soldier probably met his death at a fiercely contested stretch of land outside the walls of the old city of Jerusalem. There had been several bloody clashes there, and many Scots soldiers had been killed. They had been buried where they fell, row after row of graves marked by a simple white cross with an inscription bearing name and regiment.

Once more the territory was proving to be a flashpoint for violence between Jews and Arabs. The stretch of land had been cordoned off with barbed wire to keep the opposing forces apart. Nevertheless, shells frequently rained on and around it as a constant reminder that neither side was giving ground. There was no degree of certainty that the Scots soldier lay there. And if he did, it was unlikely that the grave would be easily located. But above all, military officials warned the minister, it was an extremely dangerous place and they strongly advised against going anywhere near it.

Currie had given his word to a mother in mourning. At dusk, when his bulky body would be a difficult target for anyone who misinterpreted his actions, he crawled through the spirals of barbed wire and entered the ground which had cost so many young lives. He walked along the rows of white crosses, examining the names of those who had fallen on this troubled soil. As the light faded, he found the young Scot's grave, and took a photograph to prove it. The heather was planted there, a little part of the lad's homeland, a mother's memorial to her son.

The remarkable story made the squabble over the Holy Water appear like a storm in a teacup. James had told no one on the pilgrimage where he had gone or what he had done that evening. When the folk of Pollok opened the pages of *The Sunday Post* he grew in their estimation.

This was the start of a lasting friendship with this newspaper in particular and many others in general. Many a reporter, myself included, who found himself staring at an empty notebook under the disapproving scowl of a grumpy news editor would once again lift a telephone and dial Currie's number, offering a silent prayer that he was at home. He was the perfect contact, a man who met people and knew what was happening to them. On the doorstep the mention of his name was an Open Sesame: 'I'm sorry to trouble you. I'm a journalist. I was speaking to the Reverend James Currie and he told me . . .'

You rarely finished the sentence. You were invited into the house, given tea and biscuits, and your host described 'what a man the minister is' and then gave chapter and verse of the story for the newspaper.

Currie was careful not to break a confidence. He would talk to the people first to find out how they felt about the story appearing in a newspaper. He elucidated the salient facts and presented them to the journalist in the correct order. All that was required was to visit the house in question and drink the tea. Many of the stories which originated from his tip-offs would be sad, sometimes tragic, and deeply personal. The people were talking to the press to 'help others, folk in similar circumstances, to help them to understand that they weren't alone.' Indeed they were not, they had Currie and his clan, and, after publication, a variety of people who telephoned or wrote in sympathy, empathy, or both.

In a sincerely felt obituary to James Currie, the editor of the *Kilmarnock Standard*, one of the journals for which he wrote, said that if James had not decided to become a minister he would have made a fine journalist. Other folk, top names in the world of entertainment, felt he was a natural for the stage – a man with a sense of timing, a presence and charisma. Farming was in Currie's blood, and when he arrived at Drumadoon the place fairly buzzed with activity. Then there were the sell-out trips to the Holy Land. The truth is that James Currie was interested in all of them and he gave to them his all. His enthusiasm was infectious and he got a great response from others.

Currie couldn't say 'No'. Particularly when things were going well, when his endeavours were appreciated and the adrenalin was pumping. Currie couldn't say 'No'. The request might come from a newspaper reporter, a television or radio producer, or an official of a group wanting to see his slides of the Holy Land. All this after serving the needs of a demanding parish. And much more.

February 1969, saw the acquisition of one of St James's greatest assets. The church was to get a new assistant minister and Margaret Flora McLean Currie, a woman who knows how to speak her mind, had left those in authority in no doubt about the qualities the man must possess in abundance. One of the prime demands was that he must be willing to work all the hours that God sends. A candidate, Ian MacKenzie, from Inverness, who was to complete his exams that May, was sent along. It will come as no surprise that James was busy, so Peggy was fully desptached to meet the new man at Queen Street station. She stood on the platform, examining the faces of those leaving the train, looking for a sign, but none came. Eventually, there were only two people left on the platform. A woman, wearing a pair of slacks and sweater that had seen better days and a young man, with fashionable, long shaggy hair. The woman introduced herself; 'I'm Peggy Currie. Are you a minister?'

Ian MacKenzie, now the minister of Garbraid Church, Maryhill, Glasgow, takes up the story.

'This was the beginning of a relationship which was to have a lasting and profound influence on my life. It was happy, busy and deeply fulfilling work assisting the Revd James Currie. The first weekend I heard James at a Burns Supper and I laughed as I never had before. But my vivid recollection of that time was Mr Currie driving along the cobbled, back streets around Broomielaw, battery shaver buzzing in one hand, *The Glasgow Herald* open on this knee, a battery-operated transistor radio in the glove compartment, and Mr Currie 'mixing a wi' admonition due.' It was a sight of bewildering activity, not to mention dangerous juxtaposition of gadgets. If they say a minister lives nearer heaven than many a one, I can only say 'yes, that's true and it shows in his driving!'

'I had no previous knowledge of Mr Currie and no prejudices to disabuse, but I did get stuck into the work and settled in very much at home with the Currie family and especially the open house at Dumbreck Road. The very first month of assistantship, in June 1969, I had seen:

A full-blown twenty-first anniversary series of services with former ministers at St James sharing in it;

Special soloists or guest artists, such as Flo Munn and the choir from Craigbank school participating;

A special service of married couples returning for thanksgiving over 21 years of marriage;

Closing assemblies in three primary schools, one secondary school and one special school;

Weddings (seven in my second weekend), funerals, and visits to the Southern General Hospital in which every parishioner from the Pollok area was culled from records and visited personally. This meant spending three afternoons in the hospital every week. Then there was the David Elder Infirmary and the Elder Cottage Geriatric Hospital . . .'

Court witness appearances in connection with a murder trial.

Ian MacKenzie spent two and a half years as assistant minister at St James's. He 'felt deeply attracted to James Currie, a warm, generous, outgoing person. He had charisma, and you felt he was interested in you as a person. He was like a father to me.'

What were his views of Currie as a minister?

'He had a dynamic quality that could only come from a personal relationship with God. His preaching, pastoral work, and personal counselling all drew their inspiration from a living, daily encounter with God. My most enduring memory of James is the weekly service of worship when he was a minister, pastor and preacher. His preaching was clear, understandable and interesting. It owed a lot to the kindred spirit of William Barclay, but was fed and flavoured by many personal experiences and the inclusion of memorable incidents from the wide variety of books he read.'

'He told stories that touched your emotions, tugged at your heart. Points of truth and application of message were made clearly and tellingly. Like Burns, he had a sharp eye for detail, and a liberal, caring heart, so that when you left church you went away enriched, blessed and uplifted – glad to be alive. The positive element which stemmed form his optimistic nature and faith in divine providence working with man's better nature shone out in his message. He told me once: 'Never have more than fifty per cent of your sermon negative or putting people down.'

'Although he read widely in religious as well as general literature, he was never one for chasing new theological fashions. He stuck to the great core of the Christian truth, making his aim to kindle or rekindle faith in the living Christ whose Spirit would make us all alive to His purpose and our mission in life. If he told once again one or two of his stories of men and women who met God in life, or were changed characters through divine grace, they were such cracking good stories that you felt anew their power as if you had heard them for the first time.

'He never tried to be cleverly intellectual, but he wanted to make the Christian faith down-to-earth, real and attractive.'

'One of the remarkable things James Currie managed to convey was a spirit of tranquillity and peace. This was all the more surprising (even unbelievable!) when you had been with him the hour or two previous to a service. The phone might have buzzed non-stop, half-eaten courses and gulps of tea punctuated by phone calls; some emergency call or folk in distress arriving for help just minutes before stepping into the pulpit; confusion, pressure and mad car dashes moments before – but once James stepped into the sanctuary the atmosphere had altered beyond recognition. Calm, unhurried grace replaced pandemonium and a spirit of worship and order blotted out noisy confusion.

'I often thought the sense of calm was as if the Lord had put his restraining hand on James's shoulder at the church door and said: "Quiet, James. Now let Me take over." '

'There was a beauty, a serenity and a relaxed sense of worship which was not matey or jarringly familiar, which had dignity but was never a cold, impersonal formality. He always wore his collar and, in services, his robes. The service had form, with the right balance of reverence and fun. The choir wore robes and added anthems or solos or instrumental accompaniment. There was mention of those who had died, followed by a musical requiem: due solemnity. But there was also a lot of good-humoured fellowship with natural laughter. He had no hesitation in taking the mickey out of his ministerial assistants, playing up their exploits in church with exaggeration that was obviously done with good humour.'

Ian remembers vividly one incident when he was the butt of the joke. In May 1970, he was on an outing to Strathhaven with a group of Sunday School children. They were boating on a pond, less than three feet deep, when a vessel carrying three girls began to sink. It was going down, with all hands on deck screaming in panic. Ian rowed to the girls, stepped into the water, and lifted the shipwrecked mariners into the 'lifeboat'. This meant there was no space for him, so he walked back to shore through (not on, he emphasised) the water. The next day Currie told the saga from the pulpit.

Ian said: 'The incident lost nothing in the telling. Three girls were drowning and a brave assistant minister risked his life to save them. By afternoon the story had been enhanced, and I had nearly lost my life. At the evening service I had all but drowned and the only thing that kept me afloat was my hair!'

Currie often referred to his young colleague by the nickname of Mod. This was not a reference to the fashionable group of the time

119

which rivalled the Rockers, but an abbreviation for James's introduction of Ian as 'the next Moderator of the General Assembly of the Church of Scotland.'

Mod was no stranger to hard work. And he found it aplenty in Pollok. When he preached his first sermon at St James's on 6 July 1969, there were no fewer than twenty-five baptisms in the kirk. In an early letter to a minister friend in Aberdeen Ian expressed amazement and enjoyment at the variety of work. He noted that in the previous few days he had visited 'a widowed mother bathing her baby, then a grandfather with a double amputation while three children were milling around.'

James Currie spoke glowingly of the younger man's talent, humanity and enthusiasm for hard work. Ian MacKenzie was proud that the man 'who was like a father to me' treated him 'not like a junior, but as a respected colleague. He would leave a lot to my discretion and took in details of situations very quickly. James's approach could be described as holistic and his philosophy was that nothing was unimportant that touched people's lives or shaped their behaviour. He said we must be as interested in the family as the church member, as attentive to worries over rent as about spiritual difficulties.'

It should be said that the Revd Ian MacKenzie is very much his own man. At Pollok, he was assistant minister, eager and happy to work for and with James Currie, but it was always known that he would pursue his own career his own way. That he has done, quietly, at Garbraid. He is unstinting in his praise of James Currie as a 'pastor, carer and spiritual counsellor who never spared himself and never hesitated to go out on calls at any time of the day or night.' Unselfishly, he passes credit to James for words of wisdom which he uses in his own ministry. 'He told me to go at once, no matter how inconvenient it might be, to a home where a death had occurred. He said "one visit that day is worth a dozen the next week or even three days later". I've never forgotten that and I have proved the value of it.'

The slight figure of Ian MacKenzie, gingery locks cascading towards his shoulders, moved smoothly through the streets of Pollok. The soft, Inverness lilt gave way to the harsher tongue of Glasgow. He learned well and he learned quickly. After a year, the usual time for an assistant to remain with a parish, his thoughts began to turn to a church of his own. But it was not yet time.

Drumadoon was one of James Currie's greatest loves. The work started by Tobago, his grandfather, and continued by his father became an obsession, a folly, and almost cost his life. James had succeeded in continuing the Currie tenancy of the farm, but he had to pay a succession of managers to run it. The land had never been rich. It yielded a living and nothing more. Currie, and his family, paid dearly for the emotional decision to retain the link of Arran. It was a constant drain on resources – body, mind and finances. In 1969, James believed that he had found a solution. He would buy Drumadoon, lock, stock and barrel. He managed to persuade his bank manager to provide the finance, a little matter of £7500, and lawyers did the rest. When he took possession of the title deeds, he became the owner of the farm, and realised the ambition of a lifetime. The young man who had been torn between the plough and the pulpit, who had wept on the rocks on the shoreline praying for guidance, now had both. The joy and satisfaction of both: the burdens and responsibilities of both. He coped with them, barely, for a few years, and then they caught up with him.

June 1970, was a glorious month. Scots spirits lifted as the country basked in blazing sunshine. On the morning of 20 June, James took a hankering to go to Arran. He was to conduct a wedding at St James's that evening, so Peggy tried to persuade him that it was not worth going to the island for a few hours but he would have none of it. Shortly after arriving at Drumadoon, she discovered the reason for the urgency. James was eager to make a start on an occupation which had long excited him, and one which would be completed on the day he died.

As a boy, he hated the rocks which lay beneath the farm's thin soil and jarred the plough and blunted its edge. Johnny, his Clydesdale, would stop at the jolt, and James would have to ease the plough over the obstacle then dig out the offending boulder and carry it to the edge of the field. This made arduous work even more difficult, and was doubly frustrating because he hated tramping over fresh furrows. Over the years, the edges of the fields became littered with these rocks. One field, known as the Doon, had seemed more stone than soil. It was one of the stretches James had reclaimed from the wild, burning bracken and heather, digging out the persistent roots, and hauling seaweed up from the shore to bind and fertilise the ground. The fence around the field had been repaired often, and would soon require to be renewed completely. But Currie had other ideas.

That fine June evening he began to gather some of the stones. He arranged them in order of size and shape: big ones, flat ones, round ones . . . Then he laid out the foundation of the beginning of one of his

121

consuming passions – a dry stane dyke. He worked slowly and methodically, trying first this rock and then that, resisting the temptation to chip parts off to fashion a stone to plug a gap. He wanted the wall literally to come out of the ground. There was a place for every stone, as there was a role for every person, it took only patience and persistence to find it. Peggy shouted to him that it was time to get washed and leave for the ferry, but he could not drag himself away. The task had a compelling fascination. After much persuasion and congratulation, Peggy finally managed to prise him away, and Charles drove them in an old car toward Brodick. The vehicle's exhaust was faulty and carbon monoxide fumes seeped up into the passenger compartment. Going down the String, a road his grandfather helped to build, James told Charles to stop the car. He got out and lay by a ditch, his head cushioned by heather, in the shadow of Goatfell. An agonising band of pain was constricting his chest. He was taking in deep, rasping breaths and his face was alarmingly pale. He asked Peggy to hold his hand.

'I'm all right. I just feel sick. Leave me for a minute,' he said.

A minute later he was worse.

Somehow Peggy and Charles lifted his twenty stones into the back of the car and drove hurriedly to the doctor in Brodick. When Peggy ran inside James insisted on getting out of the car, but he collapsed. The streets were alive with people while the minister lay on the pavement and prayed to God to let him die.

Charles said 'It was the only time I saw my mother go to pieces. But as soon as she came out of the surgery she was back in command. She told me to phone home to arrange for Ian MacKenzie to take the wedding.'

James's recollections of the events which followed were vivid. His diary records: 'Out came Dr Janice Gemmell. The pain was terrible. Dr Gemmell gave me a jag. A young lady knelt beside me and held my hand. A young man with khaki shorts held my head on his knees. Later I was to discover the girl was nurse Moira MacNiven, who had been in the doctor's surgery, and the young man Mr Wilson, Congregational minister from Rutherglen. They all kept saying "lie still", but the pain was acute.'

'The ambulance seemed to come from Lamlash quite quickly. Nurse Pam Coutts took charge. When I got to the hospital matron and her staff were waiting to greet me and to help me. Dr Wallace, by chance, was on his way to Lamlash to visit and he was at my bedside in no time. His injection helped the pain and I was soon dozing (I think I was.)

'The next five weeks are all a blur.' No visitors but Peggy and the boys. Hundreds of letters which made me weep with gratitude. Pills, pills and more pills. Great kindness from doctors, nurses and fellow patients.

'I am *glad to be alive*, and grateful to God for sparing my life.'

James had been close to death. He said later that the pain had been so acute that he had prayed to God to take him to heaven. 'I had never experienced anything like it,' he said. 'I was in agony. I couldn't think of anything but a way out of that pain. And death seemed the only way.'

The doctors in Lamlash Hospital had been so concerned about his condition that they had not undressed him for a week lest the exertion should tax his weakened heart and provoke another, perhaps fatal, coronary thrombosis. He lay fully dressed for seven days, forbidden even from lifting a glass of water. He was in hospital for more than four weeks, then taken back to Drumadoon for a further week's bed rest. He called for his diary, to record the drama of the past weeks, but Peggy had been advised not to give it to him.

He was allowed to go outside during the first week of August, but told to take only gentle walks. Work was strictly forbidden. At first this was no sacrifice because he was weak and did not feel fit enough to labour, however as his strength returned so too did the desire to work.

On the morning of 17 August Dr Runa MacKay, a doctor working at Nazareth Hospital who was back in Glasgow for a holiday, was due at Drumadoon, ostensibly for a break in the island's bracing air but really to 'Currie-sit'. Peggy, who had been his minder during the period of recuperation, caught an early ferry from Brodick to return to Dumbreck Road. Dr MacKay was to take the new Caledonia ferry from Ardrossan but the vessel ran into bad weather during her early morning voyage from Arran. Her automatic pilot jammed and she heaved over on to her side. Two lorries overturned and two cars were crushed. Seventy-seven lambs, James noted later in his diary, were suffocated. Dr MacKay was therefore delayed on the mainland and did not arrive at Drumadoon until late in the evening. The minister greeted her at the door, and she scolded him for being dirty.

'You're quite well enough to wash yourself,' she told him.

What she did not know was that Currie had taken advantage of his 'freedom' and had been out ploughing The Hill. Anyone who has sat on the metal seat of a tractor, experienced the sudden jolts as the tyres fight for traction on uneven ground, and twisted and turned to watch the plough, the line, check the ground ahead for obstacles, will tell you if this is taxing work.

James smiled sheepishly and hoped she would not come across the tractor he had deviously parked out of sight. Its tyres were still hot. The unmistakable, indescribable scent of newly turned earth wafted down on the breeze and the straight, fresh furrows looking down on them seemed to reflect the red sky. Currie was back in harness. A fortnight later, after completing a rigorous medical check-up, doctors gave permission to allow him to write up his diary. They felt he was well enough to return to an exercise book.

Ploughing, or any other form of strenuous labour, was decidedly against Dr MacKay's orders, so, over the following week, James had to content himself with bringing his diary up to date and supervising the harvest. The careful doctor was replaced as chaperon by another family friend, Ron Gouck. That evening, Currie persuaded Ron that he was permitted to walk in the high ground above Drumadoon. They were out for two hours, tramping through the most testing of ground. James had made his point. He was returning to fitness. At 8.00 am the following morning he was at a neighbouring farm borrowing a file to sharpen the reaper blades. Then he was off with two rolls of wire to construct a fence. The next day he was back on the tractor cutting corn.

James's GP, Dr Alex MacGregor, was not to 'sign him off' and so allow him to return to work until the end of October. Even then, he was strongly advised to move to a smaller church and greatly reduce his other commitments. If he picked up where he had left off he would be dead within a year. Dr MacGregor knew that the minister was working hard on the farm. He cautioned against this, but nevertheless decreed that James should remain at Drumadoon. The weight of the plough was less than that of the pulpit.

On 1 September the bulk of the text in Currie's diary is devoted to Concorde flying over Arran at 1100 mph. It was the aircraft's first supersonic flight over land, and the animals at Drumadoon were far from happy about it. The day's events are noted in order of importance. One sentence is added as an incidental: 'Peggy says Caldwell Parish Church is advertised.'

The church in Uplawmoor, Renfrewshire, had a roll about a tenth the size of St James's. Peggy was heeding the doctor's warning. She wanted James to apply for the vacancy of the small kirk. His response? Caldwell is mentioned in the diary after 'I had a lovely fire on all day. Used dross with logs.'

He did not have the slightest intention of slowing down. Indeed, he was already back serving both plough and pulpit. He conducted a christening at a church on the island and later wrote a sermon on the calf which did not recognise its mother after the cow had been dehorned . . . 'Peter did not recognise Jesus.' An STV producer telephoned to say that although James had agreed to appear for a week on 'Late Call' in October he fully understood that it would now be impossible. The word was not in Currie's vocabulary. He wrote the scripts for the appearances while at Drumadoon and one of them, 'It's Great to be Alive', about his feelings as he lay with his head on the heather fighting for life on the String, received a tremendous response.

There was one firm indicator that the minister was back to his old self and hankering to return to the fray – he started to girn at his family. Jamesie, with all the reckless irresponsibility of a man who has just qualified as a doctor, stayed out all night in the selfish pursuit of enjoying himself at a party. He was advised that he 'should look for digs.' Charles felt the sharp edge of his father's tongue for failing to collect calves from the ferry and Peggy suffered for failing to tell her son that the beasts were coming over from the mainland. Currie had 'seldom heard of such indifference and carelessness.'

The man who had felt that he could do nothing to please Drumadoon Currie was unaware that he now appeared in a similar light to his own sons. Charles had recently attained three Highers and, if his mother had had her way, would have been about to go to university to study for an arts or science degree. But he knew how much the farm meant to his father. The heart attack helped Charles to make a decision. On 5 October, he enrolled at the West of Scotland Agricultural College.

The previous day had been one of great excitement and satisfaction for James Currie. He had been back in the pulpit at St James's, preaching at both morning and evening services. The people of Pollok had heard he was coming back, although he was still 'on the panel'. The kirk's pews, which could accommodate about 1200 people, had been packed full. Chairs were brought from the church hall and placed in the aisles. Some of the elders stood at the back of the kirk. Dr MacGregor called at the manse that evening. Despite Currie's pleas he refused to allow the minister to return to work in the parish.

James's initial reaction was one of anger and frustration, then he remembered the view of the sky from the roadside on the String, the clasp of Peggy's hand in his, and the apparent certainty that he was about to die. 'I realised I was finite,' he said. The next day he went to see his lawyer 're will and arrangement of farm: it took a while. Went home and enjoyed my tea.'

Caldwell Kirk was not about to gain Currie's services, but for the first time he admitted to himself that he would have to leave St James's. The church he was to take over was just down the road from Uplawmoor, in Dunlop, which was closer to the ferry for Arran . . .

Ironically, James Currie's 'extra time' at St James's became possible because of a selfless decision by Ian MacKenzie. Much of the burdens of the parish had fallen on to those young shoulders which proved broad enough to carry them. This servant of God who had been looking to his future obediently continued to serve in Pollok as assistant minister. It is to be expected that when James became well enough to resume duties full-time, Ian should consider making a move towards taking over his own charge, but there was one further duty for him.

James outside the Currie Hall, St James.

The Cave had become a victim of its own success. Ian had taken over the running of it and, with a mix of discipline and compassion, had earned the respect and affection of its members. The premises had become too small to contain the ideology which was now recognised by the local authority. New, custom-built premises were constructed to serve as a sports and social centre. There was, James Currie said, only one man who could ensure that it was started properly.

That man, again, postponed his own plans and served. The facilities, which were named the Currie Hall, knew the benefits of this decision. Ian MacKenzie paid many tributes to James Currie. Perhaps the most meaningful was that eighteen months after his 'apprentice-ship' was over, after shining in a tough school, he chose to remain with the man 'who was like a father to me'.

CHAPTER THIRTEEN

The Holy Land

The allure of the Holy Land is great for any Christian. James Currie made forty-six visits there and was leader on pilgrimages for more than 3000 people. At the beginning of each trip, as he set foot on foreign soil, he said, 'I'm home'. Father Currie, as he was known there, twenty stones of charisma in a kilt, was adored by Jew and Arab alike.

Currie, the courier, made a fortune out of pilgrims, the cynics said. Let's lay that myth immediately. In return for recruiting members of each party, collating the organisational procedure over a period of months and acting as guide in the Holy Land, he did not have to pay for his visit. There was no wage; no commission. In fact, on numerous

A break for James and the 'Wee Yin' the Revd. Effie Irvine.

occasions, he paid for folk to go with him. Folk he had met during his widespread ministry who needed a holiday.

The trips were pilgrimages, visits to the land of the Bible, and they were happy affairs. As soon as the party had boarded a bus at the airport and Currie the microphone in his hand the vast repertoire of songs, stories and jokes would begin to unfold. He had a gift for putting people at ease. A gift, nevertheless, which required a lot of hard work. The Revd Effie Irvine, of Milton of Campsie Parish Church, Stirlingshire, who was his second-in-command on fifteen pilgrimages, testified to this.

On the flight from London James would sleep for about half of the journey waking up, with uncanny regularity, in perfect time for his meal – and often Effie's as well, 'It's not nice to waste it.' Then he would scan his list of names and set out putting faces to them. The Wee Yin, as he called Effie, would be sent to 'find out that woman's name' or 'talk to them, they look shy.' He knew the loneliness of shyness and was determined that no one on his trips would have to bow to it.

James Currie chose the title for this book, and in all my conversations with his family, friends and wide circle of contacts, his fellow minister was the first – but not the last – to describe him as a 'conman'.

'Oh, he was a conman all right,' Effie said. 'And a great one. He conned everyone, got them to do exactly as he wanted. He did it with hotel owners and managers, guides, drivers and pilgrims too. He got them to do exactly as he wished – conned them year after year – and the trips were all the better for it.'

Currie 'at home' had his flock eating out of his hand. People wanted to please the man who tried so hard to please them. They gave as much as they took. Quite simply, he brought out the best in them, and sometimes that was just as well. The popularity of his pilgrimages, and his reluctance to put up the house full sign, often meant that there was an acute shortage of accommodation at hotels. People who had been assured that they would have a single room found that they would have to share. Currie knew this. Show me the package tour holidaymaker who has not experienced an administrative blunder and I will show you the exception. The inconvenience and annoyance over being 'swindled' generally leads to an exchange of angry words. Effie watched year after year as 'James turned on those big eyes and said "I know, I know, but you've got to help me. It's terrible, I know, but please help me," and folk ended up sharing rooms with complete strangers. He conned them. Time and again.'

Currie, of course, was a well-known face. Many of the people who went on the pilgrimages did so largely to spend some time listening to his repartee. The lady minister was not so well-known, but James would always introduce her with a chuckle: 'This is the Reverend Euphemia H C Irvine and I taught her all she knows.'

The overcrowding arose because of one of James greatest failings which was at the same time one of his most endearing qualities. He could not say 'No'. There was always time for one more pilgrim. A few days before one trip was due to leave he telephoned the manse in Milton of Campsie to inform his lieutenant that the party had expanded.

'How many are going now?' Effie asked.

'One hundred and six.'

'Oh James, if there are any more we'll have to drive the buses.'

'So what.'

If it had been his only way of getting to the Holy Land he would have done it.

During one visit the have-to-share ploy rebounded on him. Every good con requires its actors to play their part in 'The Sting'. When the party arrived at the Panorama Hotel in Jerusalem, horror of horrors, golly what a surprise, there was a shortage of single rooms. Dr Eileen McIlroy, a Scot now living in York and a veteran of sixteen Currie pilgrimages, stood with Peggy and Panorama owner Joseph Aweida, waiting for her cue.

Currie: '. . . it's terrible, I know, but you've got to help me. We'll share a room too. We'll share with . . .'

(Looks around, expressing eagerness to share a room with any available doctor with the name of McIlroy who has been a family friend for years)

'. . . Peggy and I will share with Dr McIlroy. Do *you* mind sharing, Dr McIlroy?'

(Gasps of astonishment from other Sting actors.)

'Not at all,' the doctor replies, 'it's the only way so let's make the best of it.'

(Joseph Aweida's admiration stops just short of applause. Undercurrent of rhubarb, rhubarb as supporting actors signify willingness to share and share alike. Extras, caught up in the spirit of things, respond on the double.)

The pilgrims went in two by two.

At this stage, however, the plot takes a twist and begins to resemble a Brian Rix farce.

(Exit the minister, his wife, and the lady doctor to their communal boudoir.)

Dr McIlroy dons nightdress and dressing gown in the adjoining bathroom and goes to her bed. Currie, meanwhile, has discreetly disrobed and is in his bed. Both fall sound asleep while Peggy reads.

(There is a gentle knock on the door. The bedroom door. There are no french windows in the Panorama Hotel. Enter Attractive Young Pilgrim.)

AYP: 'Verily, I hath been offered a lift to Bethlehem in the chariot of an Amorous Young Arab and I would dearly like to go. Peggy, I prithee, come with us, lest his intentions be less than honourable.'

(Peggy looks warily at sleeping husband and doctor. Places back of hand to brow in classic pose of dilemma. Finally casts aside thoughts of rude awakenings, and picks up chaperone's cloak. Lights dull. Some three hours later, somewhat disappointed AYA drops relieved AYP and Peggy at Panorama. Lights rise a little in boudoir. Sounds of peaceful sleep coming from bed of doctor. Agitated, very much awake, gasps escape from the minister's blankets. Peggy tip-toes into boudoir. She is only one to hear minister's soliloquy.)

There is insufficient space in this volume to record the words verbatim, or even to give a résumé. Suffice to say that sentences begin with: 'How could you; What on earth; What would people; and Never have I been so . . .' Occasionally, there is a suggestion of a woman's muted chuckle. Backs are turned after the words, 'Och James, would you wheesht.'

Eventually, the pilgrims went to sleep. Three by three.

Currie hated what he called read prayers, texts which were prepared in advance and adhered to strictly. He wanted all of the people in his party to read from the Bible. Those were too shy, or simply did not want to, had only to see him to be excused. Many saw him. None was excused. He believed that spontaneous prayers related more closely to the occasion and people could relate to them. Effie discovered this during her first pilgrimage when their party visited the Upper Room where Christ served the Last Supper to his disciples. James conducted a service and then informed the pilgrims that Effie would say the prayer.

'I was astounded,' she said. 'He just landed it on me. But he was right. I was hesitant at first but the prayer did have a relevant meaning. If you know your Bible and your people the right words just come. And James Currie knew his Bible. Just mention any passage and he could open the Bible right at it.'

Resting at Masada.

One of the most moving moments was with a woman who knew she was dying of cancer. She was extremely weak, restricted to a wheelchair and could visit few places, but James insisted on special arrangements so she could make the trip. The woman was restricted to her bed on many days, but the minister always visited her for what Effie described as 'deeply moving prayers. That woman went to the Holy Land to reaffirm her faith. James Currie helped her to do that. She was at peace.'

One elderly woman's determination to see the Holy Land almost cost her life. She suffered from a serious blood disorder and had to attend hospital regularly for tests to ensure that her blood was not clotting or conversely becoming 'too thin'. Samples of her blood were examined and drugs dispensed with extreme caution to maintain the correct balance. However, since her hospital appointment fell in the middle of the pilgrimage she chose to ignore it.

On a hilly wall outside Nazareth, Effie noticed the woman lagging behind the rest of the party. She watched the woman's progress carefully and then saw that there were blotches, like bruises, on her legs. Fortunately, Ellen Pollok, senior nursing officer at the Victoria Infirmary, Glasgow, and another veteran of the Currie pilgrimages, was at hand. Ellen knew immediately that there was something seriously wrong and confronted the woman who explained her predicament. She was taken to hospital immediately and detained until her condition could be stabilised.

The woman had not taken out insurance against illness. Indeed, had she attempted to her secret would have got out and her trip would almost certainly have been cancelled. A rapid whip-round was arranged to pay her medical bills.

When the pilgrimage ended in Jerusalem, James went to the hospital to check if the woman could return home with them. Doctors explained that she was too weak to travel and would have to remain in hospital for a further two weeks.

Effie said: 'He set out on the hour's journey to Nazareth by taxi around midnight and did not get back until 3.00 am. He could have telephoned, but that wouldn't do. He had to see the woman to assure her that we were thinking about her. Our flight left at 4.30 am and he hadn't even packed his bags.'

When the woman was allowed to return to Scotland James ensured that she was met at the airport. He visited her at home after that and arranged for others to call on her at regular intervals.

Currie in the Holy Land made the Bible an open book. His deep knowledge and understanding of the scriptures along with his talent as a raconteur brought the stories to life. The 'Minister' from the playground had seen Moses return with the tablets from the Doon and the Red Sea part in Blackwaterfoot Bay, and in the land where these events actually happened, his knowledge and vivid imagination painted word pictures that all but brought the occasions to life. One afternoon, however, his powers of description and persuasion back-fired.

Hurry Currie he was called. It became the rallying cry that everyone used to muster the troops. When it was time to return to the coach it was Hurry Currie. If anyone dallied they were told to Hurry Currie. Even waiters in restaurants trying to serve 150 people at once responded to the Hurry Currie command. There was so much to see and so little time that he was always rushing folk along. One day he realised, with something approaching horror, that the party had a free afternoon. Effie, informed of this sacriligious outrage, dared to venture the opinion that the folk would appreciate the rest. Many of them were elderly and feeling the effects of hilly walks in the hot climate.

'You didn't disagree with James,' Effie stated firmly, 'he was right – and he was – and would do things his way. But I spoke to the people and what they wanted was a wee rest. I tried to persuade James, but he wouldn't hear of it.'

The waste of time was 'shocking'. Folk could sit about and talk at home. They'd come to see the Holy Land and see the Holy Land they would. He was roused to something close to anger, but when he spoke to folk there was not a trace of it. The wordsmith wove his silver web. There was a place, oh what a place, where there was a volcano with a pool of water that was the purest blue and the sky was clear and the view from the hilltop was the closest thing to heaven . . . would they come, oh why wouldn't they come? Currie was going, oh, he wanted to go so much, would they help him . . .? They helped him. Two busloads helped him.

As the buses climbed up the hill the mist fell down. The pilgrims could see nothing. Leaving the coaches would have been foolish in the extreme. Charlie, one of the drivers, described the situation perfectly. He rolled down his window, put out a hand and said, 'We are in London?' The humorous respite was short-lived. The drive up the steep road, round hairpin bends which looped falls of hundreds of feet, was arduous in the best of conditions. In well-nigh zero visibility it was a nightmare. Charlie, and his colleague, did it 'to help Father

Currie.' When they eventually managed to turn the buses around and crawl back down the drivers had to exercise great caution. There were other vehicles, ponderous, heavy machinery from the sound of them, climbing relentlessly. At one bed, where a puff of wind dispersed the mist, the folk in the buses saw one of the many vehicles in the convoy. It was an Israeli tank, making its way up the hill, otherwise known as the Golan Heights. The pilgrims had not seen the view that was the closest thing to heaven, but they understood why life today in the Holy Land can be nearer to hell.

James Currie was a member of a broad Church. He hated 'narrow-minded churchianity which has nothing to do with Christianity.' His down-to-earth approach and eagerness to take the Church to the people was mistaken by some as shallowness but the ministers who knew him best scorn those who advocate this theory as suffering from shallowness themselves. Ian MacKenzie spoke of Currie's serenity, his ability to step out of the commotion which was so much part of his everyday life and conduct religious services with calmness and assurance. He brought peace to troubled hearts.

During a visit to the Holy Land one man told James that he had not become a member of a church because he had not been baptised. Currie decided to put that to rights and the service is captured on video film. The party made a special trip to the River Jordan and, wearing swimming trunks, the man and the minister waded into the murky water. The sharply falling river bed is dangerous and strewn with sharp stones, so they took a walking stick for balance. There was a shaky road bridge near the spot and every time a car passed over it the sound of the pilgrims singing a hymn on the banks is almost drowned. Nevertheless, the atmosphere is one of peace and serenity. On another occasion James baptised a woman in the Jordan. She bought a long, flowing white dress for the occasion which was 'absolutely beautiful'.

'James had a gift for creating a perfect atmosphere,' Effie said. 'He helped many people to find their faith and many more to retain it.'

A pilgrimage with Currie and the Wee Yin was a recipe for hilarity, often unscripted slapstick. James, coyly undressing under trees at the Dead Sea and donning trunks which might have accommodated the Nautilus in dry dock, was always a highlight. Veteran visitors knew that they had to wait until the tidal wave subsided to snap a picture of the 'stranded whale' floating on his back.

Effie too, provided mirth on more than one occasion. During one of the longer drives she felt compelled to answer the call of nature.

'But Wee Yin,' James chided, 'there's only the occasional acacia tree out there.'

Undaunted, the Revd Effie replied: 'Aye, but it's acacia desperate need!'

On another occasion, in a restaurant, one elderly woman who had contracted a tummy bug had what is best described was a wee accident. Peggy, ever-practical, knew that Effie was wearing slacks. She sent James to ask the Wee Yin to sacrifice her nether garments. Effie treated the request diplomatically.

'Naw, I'm no' taking my breeks off for any man. Not even James Currie.'

At this stage, I will kill the scandal that shocked the members of one pilgrimage and reveal the identity of the drunken women pilgrims. Or rather, the women pilgrims who were not drunk, no, that's not right either . . . let me start at the beginning.

After bathing in the Dead Sea one lady retired early to her room. She said she was feeling tired, but about midnight Effie was awakened by a telephone call. The lady needed her assistance. Effie found her in tears, clutching a towel to her eye. She wouldn't let the minister examine her face, but, in faltering sobs explained her predicament. She had a glass eye and the salt from the Dead Sea had irritated the socket. She had removed the eye and placed it on the wash basin while she bathed her face. Unfortunately, her arm had nudged the eye and flipped it into the basin. Worse was to follow. She had pulled out the plug and there was no protective mesh over the hole. Her eye had disappeared, hopefully to lodge in the S-bend under the sink. If only they could remove it. This was a two-woman job, so Effie telephoned Eileen.

And that was why at midnight, with a housecoat over her pyjamas, Effie stood at the main reception desk trying in sign language to indicate to the night porter whose only word of English was 'hello' that she needed a spanner to remove an S-bend to retrieve a glass eye.

'Hello?'

'An eye.'

Points to an eye.

'Hello?'

'Down the sink.'

Ever got a sink in charades?

'Hello?'

'The S-bend.'

S is easy. Bend is . . .

'Hello?'

And that was why at midnight, with a housecoat over her pyjamas, Effie led the night porter whose only word of English was 'hello' to the lift and thence to the bedroom where Eileen was trying to console the unfortunate lady. Effie demonstrated to the young Arab that a spanner was required. he returned with the tool but, in his zealous attempts to loosen the large nut on the S-bend, succeeded only in dislodging the basin from the wall. This was accompanied by a great deal of noise. The young man, deposited unceremoniously on his rear with a thud, made a loud noise. The agitated lady made a louder noise. In time, and after more noise, the S-bend was removed and the eye plopped on to the floor. After it had been safely deposited in a glass of disinfectant, the Revd and the Doc made their way back to their rooms.

The humour of the situation overcame them. They made laughing noises.

Currie slept through it all, blissfully ignorant of the drama.

In the morning, Effie joined him for breakfast.

'Go and chat to those two ladies, Wee Yin,' he told her. 'They've hardly spoken to anyone.'

Effie is seldom short of small talk, but each avenue of conversation she opened was rapidly closed off. Finally, one of the women raised a fresh topic.

'There's one thing worse than drunks and that's drunken women. And on a pilgrimage!'

Effie was lost for words. The night porter, just going off duty, winked at her and said, 'Hello.'

That was one of the few incidents which took place without James being involved. Father Currie ran his parties like a crossing between a mother hen and a regimental sergeant major. One woman, to her great regret, incurred the full force of his wrath. She meticulously kept notes of each place the group visited but on a journey between Eilat and Jerusalem she ran out of paper. She wanted a new notebook. James explained that there were no shops and offered pages from his own pad but that would not do. She wanted a new notebook. The bus made a special stop, and Joseph Aweida, the prosperous owner of the Panorama, offered to try to find a notebook for her. However, he was unsuccessful and Hurry Currie called a halt to search. He got on the front bus and ordered the woman to take her seat with Effie in the following one. Mr Aweida apologised to the woman for his failure to help. She replied that she expected nothing better from 'a wog'. There is no bigger insult to an Arab gentleman, and Effie heard it. She raced after James and told him about the incident.

'I've never seen him move so fast,' Effie said. 'He was absolutely furious. He grabbed the woman by the scruff of the neck and practically dragged her to Joseph and made her apologise.'

James was, indeed, furious. He was also deeply hurt.

He said, 'This woman, who had the cheek to call herself a Christian, was a disgrace. To do that, to say a thing like that, and supposed to be on a pilgrimage. And poor Joseph, a gentleman, a prosperous respected man. To be insulted like that. I just told her. I told her straight. I don't think I've ever encountered such ignorance and insensitivity.'

Currie lost his temper on one other occasion in the Holy Land. As he strolled among the bazaars in Jerusalem his wallet was visible in the back pocket of his trousers. A young Arab boy attempted to steal it, but the ample upholstery around the Currie rear prevented a swift snatch. James felt the movement and turned swiftly, swinging a hefty forearm. It caught the boy on the top of his head and hasted his already speedy departure.

'All night he was so worried,' Effie said. 'He kept on saying "what if I've hurt him" over and over again. He really upset himself. I tried to tell him that the boy was a thief and it was an occupational hazard, but he wouldn't be consoled.'

There was another time when Currie's welfare gave cause for concern. Effie saw him sitting alone in a church while the members of the party were strolling about the building.

'I knew it wasn't like him but, well, I was afraid to ask if he was all right. He had a sharp tongue, you know. It was his party and he did things his way. But the more I looked the more I realised that something was wrong. And then I began to get flustered, so I decided to take the bull by the horns. I went to him and saw that he was a pale grey colour. There were beads of sweat standing out on his face, and I thought he was having another heart attack. So I said – James Currie, are you having a heart attack? He looked at me and said:

'No, but I've got diarrhoea!'

He spent the remainder of the day in isolated contemplation. The fruit of the vine had been his downfall. He had been afflicted on previous trips, the world falling out of his bottom, but he never learned. The grapes of wrath . . .

Currie was a boozer. He poured it away like there was no

tomorrow. Oh, he disguised it in orange juice, but he took a good bucket. Friends of James Currie would hear these claims from people who had 'seen him at it'. There is not a fluid ounce of truth in these stories. James Currie was teetotal, and he hated alcohol, not just the abuse of it, but its very existence. He had seen so many families split up by drink, so many men, and women, whose lives were ruined that he detested the stuff.

As he lay in his hotel room contemplating another visit to the lavatory, Effie entered with 'medicine'.

She said, 'I always take a miniature of brandy with me for exactly this type of malady. I knew James's views on alcohol, so I tried to force him to take two teaspoons of brandy. He was really quite ill, but he looked up and said – I'd rather die.'

There was high drama during one visit to the Dead Sea. An elderly lady from the group was spotted floating face down. She was rescued by Israeli soldiers and Ellen Pollok administered first aid. The ambulance was on the spot quickly and Ellen accompanied the woman to hospital, working desperately to try to ensure that all the water was out of her stomach. The Dead Sea has a high concentration of minerals, particularly magnesium carbonate, which can cause serious medical complications. The ambulance driver understood the urgency and wasted no time in the journey over bumpy, twisting roads. Ellen was tossed around like a cork in a storm. At one stage the restraining bar on the woman's makeshift bed collapsed, and Ellen had to hold on to her to prevent her from being thrown on to the floor of the vehicle. By the time they arrived at the hospital Ellen sported several painful bruises, including a black eye. Fortunately, the lady recovered, due largely to Ellen's quick thinking and medical expertise.

The administration and organisation of up to 120 pilgrims was a never-ending task which required assiduous dedication. Effie was impressed by Currie's calm approach and the way he took responsibility.

'It wasn't an easy job,' he said. 'Imagine collecting £7 from each of 120 people for a trip, holding the cash, and paying for buses, meals, other costs and dispensing tips as well. All the time he was talking, his mind a step ahead, planning what we would do next. There was a steady stream of repartee and frequent warnings "that if you're behind the Wee Yin you're lost." He was a brilliant man.'

On one occasion that brilliance dimmed. James was in charge of a party which landed at Amman for a pilgrimage in Jordan. The Arabs did not allow anyone whose passport bore an Israeli stamp into their country. James emphasised this point with the members of his group when he made final travel arrangements. The travel firm had provided special forms which entitled folk to obtain a fresh passport. Currie emphasised the importance of this. He was well aware of the distrust which existed between the two nations, and always asked Israeli Customs officers not to stamp his passport.

'That was all very well for him,' Eileen said, 'he towered over the counter and could see what they were doing. But for the likes of Effie and myself, who need ladders to reach public telephones, once the passports were out of our hands they could have been playing noughts and crosses on them. When I examined my passport it did, indeed, have an Israeli stamp so I applied for, and received a second one.'

After the aircraft touched down at Amman, Alastair McCabe, the travel agent, collected the passports of all members of the party and took them to officials at Jordanian Customs. He returned, solemn faced, and broke the news to the pilgrims that two members of the party had defied the golden rule. Their documents had Israeli stamps. A woman realised immediately that she had handed over the wrong passport and immediately proferred the correct one.

'Who's the other one?' Currie asked sternly. He knew the inconvenience the red tape would cause.

'It's you,' Alastair informed him.

James, of course, was not to blame. As usual, he had been busy tending to the needs of others and had not made the time to look after himself. That had been left to Peggy, and she had not seen one stamp from Ben Gurion airport. The remainder of the group left for their hotel at 7.00 pm, while their leader tried to explain away the mix-up to disgruntled Jordanian officials. He was allowed to deposit his baggage at the hotel around 9.00 pm then he was whisked off to the British Embassy. The ambassador, who had been attending an official function, was not best pleased at being disturbed. However, photographs were taken of the shame-faced minister and a fresh passport was issued.

He was allowed to check into the hotel at 1.00 am and was sent to bed without any dinner.

The problems over visiting an Arab land also exposed much of what Currie disliked about 'narrow-minded ministers who turn people away from the Church.'

A prominent businessman from the West of Scotland had won a major civil engineering contract in an Arab country. The real value of the deal was that it could lead to further lucrative business, so he rearranged a busy schedule to make time to visit the country and get the work off the ground himself. There was only one snag. To work there he had to have a minister sign a document to prove that he was a Christian – that is, proof that he was not Jewish.

The man went to his local minister, explained the situation, and asked if he would sign the document. The minister refused, saying that since the businessman was not a member of his church he could not testify that he was a Christian. He asked if the man had been married in a church. He had. Then, said the clergyman, he should get the minister of that church to sign the document.

The man was frustrated and upset. However, he went back to church where he had been married only to find that it had a new minister. When asked if he would put his name to a form to enable a Scottish businessman to work in the Middle East, he suggested that the man go to his local church . . .

James said, 'What a disgrace. A respectable and respected man felt humiliated after shocking treatment by two small-minded bureaucrats. They must have felt justified in their actions because the man was not a member of the Church. But surely the minister's job is to try to bring people into the Church, not turn them away from it. I did not know the man personally, but I knew his reputation. I signed his form gladly. After all, it was only a piece of paper.'

In April, 1986, James Curire made his forty-fifth visit to the Holy Land. It was his intention, or so he said, to 'retire' as guide after his fiftieth trip. Effie knew that he could reach that figure within three years, yet she found herself in a baker's shop in Tiberius ordering a chocolate covered cake with the figure forty-five on it.

'I don't know why I did it,' she said, 'but I'm glad I did. We had a waiter bring it into the dining room in the hotel after our evening meal. When James saw it he cried like a big boy. There was a lot of boy in him. He just wept and the tears rolled down his cheeks.'

There was a bond between the big boy and his Wee Yin. When Effie's husband, Alex, was suffering from a terminal illness Currie 'ministered to him for six months. James took the funeral service and it was moving.'

Currie was a great support of the Kirk's first female minister to have her own charge. Effie was ordained sixteen years ago, at the age of forty-eight. Currie was among the first to congratulate her, and the two remained firm friends. In October 1986, when he started making arrangements for the following April's visit to the Holy Land, James telephoned the manse in Milton of Campsie. He was upset, and wanted Effie to make a pledge.

'If I can't make that visit promise me you'll take it.'

Effie knew James's sensitivities and moods. She tried to console and joke, but Currie was adamant.

'Promise me, Effie, that's all, promise me you'll lead the group.'

She promised, and it seemed to put him at ease. On 23 March, James called at her manse unannounced. He had 'just been passing'. Effie had been presiding over a meeting of her presbytery records. James accepted the offer of a cup of tea. He drank it, large overcoat buttoned, scarf still knotted around his neck, and then he broached his business.

He said to the session clerk: 'I need her to come to the Holy Land with me. Please let her come. I need her.'

Effie reminded him that she was to lead a party of pilgrims at the end of the month. He was really asking her to leave her parishioners again within ten days. it simply wasn't possible. Neither the Currie charm nor the big boy's pleadings could move her.

Earlier, he had telephoned Eileen in York and pleaded with her to accompany him. She, too, was unable to do so.

Within a month James Currie was dead.

If he had made that pilgrimage, that final visit to his 'home', he wanted to have a minister and a doctor with him. Peggy always cautioned James before he went on a pilgrimage to take things easy. She knew well that he would do too much and was concerned for his health. James told her he would be happy to die in the Holy Land.

When James Currie was cremated, on 21 April, one dear friend was missing from the service. She was leading a party of pilgrims in the Holy Land.

Effie said: 'Half of the people there had never met James but they were there because of him. It was James they really wanted to see. The first two days were a real greetin' meetin'. On the third day we were on a bus leaving Jerusalem when I heard James say, 'Come on – get on with it.' Forty years earlier, when faced with the heartbreaking task of trying to remove a boulder from the Doon field, James had heard his father say, 'James, you're not going to give up now . . .'

So Effie switched on the microphone and said, 'He's gone. There have been sad days but the sad days are over. James Currie's there on cloud nine and he's saying "Get on with it". Here's some of the things he would have told you.'

And she told some Currie stories, 'not the way he told them, not as

Currie the pedlar, with Ibrahim.

good as he told them, but it was what they wanted to hear.'

One of the highlights of each trip was a visit to a bazaar in Bethany. Ibrahim, a stall owner, and James put on a double act. Currie would 'sell' the goods, forcing folk to barter with him.

'No, no. That too cheap. I got many children. Need plenty money.'

Effie and Eileen were in their hotel in April when they were summoned to the reception desk. Ibrahim was waiting for them.

'Father Currie? He is not here? It is true?' he asked.

Effie confirmed that James was dead.

'He broke down and wept. He was shaking violently and could not be consoled,' she said.

Another trader, who had a stall outside the Church of the Primacy, had also heard the news. When Effie's group stopped there he did not attempt to sell anything, but when it left he raced after them and gave

Effie a bag bursting with souvenirs. 'For you,' he said. 'For Father Currie . . . for Father Currie.'

A boy, aged about ten, who sold orange juice outside the Garden of Gethsemane, also ran after the group. Effie said, 'He recognised me, but it was James he was looking for. He kept saying "but where is Father Currie?" He walked away with tears in his eyes.'

Whenever James's group visited a kibbutz at Eingave, Ben Joseph, an eighty-year-old guide, would make a special effort and take charge of a tour. When one of the kibbutz members saw Effie as the bus arrived, he ran to fetch the old man. Ben Joseph had not been well. Father Currie was just the tonic he needed. Effie, again, had to break the bad news. Ben Joseph did not come out.

The elderly owner of a restaurant would welcome James's parties with the words, 'Now be good children. Eat your meal and you will get a sweet.' He loved the game as much as James. The man's son was delighted when he saw Effie. His father, too, was ill. Father Currie was just the tonic he needed. But Father Currie was not there. When he was told that James had died the old man went to his bed. When Effie returned nine months later, he had died. 'He had been grieving for James,' she said.

A photographer used to climb the hill to take photographs of members of the party. 'No more,' he said, 'not without Father Currie.'

Joseph, a guide, saw Effie leading the party on to an aircraft at Aqaba, Jordan, to return home. 'His eyes lit up and he scanned the group for James,' she said. I had to tell him that James was dead. And this big man just cried. Tears rolled down his cheeks.

'The Holy Land holds tremendous memories of James Currie. He is irreplaceable. There will never be another like him. He was a big man in every sense of the word. When he introduced me to people the words he used were only a joke but he was right, this is the Reverend Euphemia H C Irvine, and he taught me all I know.'

CHAPTER FOURTEEN

Burns suppers

James Currie was proud to be described as popular. The dictionary definition of the word is: of the people; generally liked or admired. He certainly saw himself as an 'ordinary' man, a common five-eighths. Perhaps his popularity and admiration of his talents was best displayed on the Burns Supper circuit. He was the most sought-after speaker in Scotland and, for those who like extravagant phrases, the most popular authority on Burns in the world. This aspect of his life, as in many others, was generally liked – but there were critics.

A criticism, seldom made to his face, was that a man of God should find little to praise in the irresponsible, drunken philanderer. Currie, on the other hand, had a place in his heaven for the man, and love in his heart for his work.

James was brought up with Burns's words on Drumadoon. His parents were devotees, and in his primary school days he already knew by heart some of the bard's works. His parents, remember, were good, God-fearing folk, and they were farmers, as Burns was a farmer, from a Christian home.

It is a familiar theme – the plough and the pulpit.

James's first Burns Supper, albeit in the informal surroundings of his Aunt Janey's home in Corriecravie, also went a long way towards forming an early opinion – the hatred of the abuse of alcohol.

James's first request to speak at a Burns Supper came when he was at West Pilton, 'I was terrified and I didn't think I was very good, but I was asked to speak at another and, well, it just took off from there. It all happened by accident – perhaps that should be the title of the book – I didn't look for any of it. I didn't look for any of it. I certainly never asked to speak anywhere but my diary's pretty full.'

Currie certainly was in demand. He received around 1500 requests a year to speak at functions but could accept fewer than 20 per cent. There were simply not enough nights in the year. In total, he spoke at more than two thousand Burns Suppers, forty-nine in one year alone. Many people 'booked early to avoid disappointment', so there were entries in his diaries for years to come. Peggy told him was tempting

Glasgow Herald

A Burns Supper and Currie in full flow . . .

fate, but he said that was not his problem. When he died, in April 1987, his diary was crammed with appointments. The following year's Burns season was fully booked, with reservations around Burns night until 1991.

Currie's talents brought requests to speak all over the globe. He proposed the Immortal Memory in Chicago, Winnipeg, Edmonton, Kuwait, Nigeria, Bahrain, Denmark, all over the United Kingdom and for a live television broadcast on a ferry crossing from Stranraer to Larne! He enjoyed the opportunities to see different parts of the world, to meet different people, but he had no doubt about which Burns Supper was the most important. 'It's definitely the next one,' he said. 'And then it will be the one after that.' His approach was the same whether he was addressing 2500 people in a grand hall in Chicago, where the haggis was piped in by two pipe bands, or speaking to a handful of old folk in a home. Had he turned down requests to speak at prestigious functions because of prior engagements? 'Dozens, oh hundreds. The work of the parish comes first. If there's a funeral sometimes I have to cancel. But if I'm free it's first-come first-served!'

Before every speech, Currie was a bag of nerves. Peggy said: 'You just couldn't talk to him. It was the same on a Sunday before church.' The nerves are evident as he rises to his feet at the Burns Supper. There is a slight tremor in the voice, a hesitancy. But the professional goes on. The adrenalin is pumping. Then he gets his 'fix', the first laugh. And he needs more . . .

But Currie 'murdered Burns – it was twenty-five minutes of Oor Jimmy and five minutes of Rabbie.' So where did his popularity spring from?

There were initial, almost mandatory protestations of bemusement followed by his explanation. 'Maybe the way I put it over has something to do with it. I try to be amusing – but there's a point to every story. But I've no time for the folk who think that Burns Suppers should be sombre, solemn affairs. I call them the double-bass face brigade. Rabbie wasn't like that. He liked to laugh.'

There was the man who sat through an entire speech and never cracked a smile. His friend asked, 'What's wrong, do you no' think he's funny.' The man with the double-bass face replied, 'Aye, he's funny, but I don't like him. I'll laugh when I go home.'

Currie's audiences certainly laughed. His favourite opening was, 'Since this is a Burns Supper it is not inappropriate to begin with Miss Raquel Welch . . .' To cut a long story short, she shred various flimsy items of clothing while a man was cleaning the windows of hotel in which she was staying in Scotland. James declined to go into a detailed description of her anatomy because 'I am a minister and no' a doctor.' Eventually, the man asked, in a Glasgow accent, 'Whit's the matter wi' you . . . huv ye no' seen a windae cleaner before?'

Currie follows this with 'and judging by the looks I've been getting some of you haven't seen a minister before.'

As ever, he is wearing his clerical collar. It is his first reference to religion, and there are more to come.

At this stage he calls for two minutes silence for the Celtic football team. It is not the last reference to Celtic.

The Immortal Memory he liked best was recorded on tape at Canmore Golf Club, in the 1970s. The beginning of the event was delayed because of confusion over an unexpected deficiency of seats. The event had been sold out for weeks, but it seemed that the mathematics had gone wrong. It transpired that a number of tickets had been forged! I've taken many people to court but that's the first time I've driven folk to crime,' he said.

He spoke authoritatively on Burns the ploughman, poet, philosopher and philanthropist. The speech was, in fact, ten minutes Currie and twenty minutes Burns. Strictly speaking, Currie lasted approximately eight minutes. Laughter and applause took up the remainder. Since this book is on the life of the former, let me tell you about some of those eight minutes.

'I'm just back from a visit to the Holy Land. One woman who was there with me went into hospital for a heart operation the week after we came back. The doctor didn't want her to make the pilgrimage, but she said she was going because "you can never be sure." I drove her to the hospital and heard the doctor ask, "Is Mr Currie your minister?" She replied: "Naw. He's jist a man I go on holiday with".'

Then there is the girl sitting on a luggie stool trying to milk a cow. 'She's chug-chug-chugging away and getting nowhere fast. Then the cow said to her, "Jist you haud ticht, lassie, an' I'll jump up an' doon".'

There is also steel in the speech. Radio 3 and *The Glasgow Herald* Arts pages are criticised for 'pandering to intellectual snobbery, and ranting over incomprehensible nonsense which starts nowhere, goes nowhere and gets lost in between.' Burns is not like that. His genius lies in stating how we all feel in ordinary language. 'Deep calleth unto deep.' The 'shallow' Bertrand Russell is put down for suggesting that if you get the wage packet right everything else will follow. Billy

Graham, who 'promised heaven on earth for repentant sinners' is reminded 'that there is a cross at the heart of everything – Christ said lift up your cross and follow Me.'

There is a critical appraisal of Burns the man, and society today, but above all, there is laughter. Currie's 'feel' for the audience is good. He assesses the mood with the first few jokes and tailors his repertoire accordingly. He has several routines, and is professional enough to know when to alter tack. He has been on stage with Tarbuck . . .

One criticism which hurt him deeply was that Currie told dirty stories. 'Never, never, have I told a dirty joke. I wouldn't dream of getting laughs like that. I don't like dirty stories anyway. If I had to sink to that I'd pack it in.' His stories were about people and the things people did. 'I never told a story that I wouldn't repeat in front of my grandchildren.' Then he laughs, 'Mind you, I got some of them from my grandchildren!'

Peggy and her family were deeply hurt when a man from a publishing company called at the manse not long after her husband's death and asked if he could publish, 'James's joke book.' He was sent packing. Peggy said, 'What an awful way that would have been for James to be remembered. Of course he told jokes, but he did it to make a point. Every joke had a purpose, whether it was to emphasise a point or lead him into a new topic. Anyway, James didn't have a "joke book". They were written on scraps of paper and the like.'

One woman in Pollok rebuked James telling a risqué joke. 'It was my Frankie Vaughan story of all things,' he said. 'I'd just gone to Pollok, knocked on a door and the man said "Oh my, you're awfy like Frankie Vaughan," so I told him not to be disrespectful. I'm your new minister. At the next door, an old woman said "Jings, you're awfy like Frankie Vaughan." Now, that's enough of that. I'm your new minister. The third door was opened by a young thing in a flimsy negligée and she said "My goodness, you're awfy like Frankie Vaughan." And I sang Give Me the Moonlight . . .'

The Revd Jimmy Dow of Lochranza, was one of James's greatest friends, and the willing butt of many of his jokes. Currie was a fine mimmick, and he took off Jimmy Dow, 'who had gravel with his cornflakes,' perfectly. 'And he would stand in the pulpit at Pirnmill Kirk and with that great mathematical brain would calculate exactly the amount on the collection plates – £4.38p. – He was delighted, because the collection was usually £4.35p. And he said, 'Well, brethren, I see we have a visitor in our midst.' And a wee man from High Valleyfield stood up and said: 'What dae ye mean wan visitor – there's three o' us!'

It's an old joke. It's not a very funny joke. It was the way Currie told them . . . His timing was great. The punchline would be delivered like a machine gun rattle and the laughter would not have died when he set out of the next one. The 'visitors in our midst' would be from a town or village with a contingent at the supper. He would 'tell stories slowly in case there are any Edinburgh folk here.' A section of the audience would howl mock anger. 'Oh, sorry, I meant Leith folk.' Someone always rose to the bait. 'That's worse, I'm from Leith.' He knew who came from Leith. The rapport is evident and important. The people at the supper are no longer an audience but participants. They're contributing to the entertainment. They're helping to entertain themselves. Currie had them eating out of the palm of his hand.

And while he had them, he delivered his message. He genuinely loves Burns's works, and quotes them often in the pulpit. The patriotic Scot is fiercely proud of the patriotic Scot:

> From scenes likes these old Scotia's grandeur springs,
> That makes her lov'd at home, rever'd abroad:
> Princes and lords are but the breath of kings,
> An honest man's the nobles work of God;

The fine minds of sheriffs, doctors and university professors who speak on the Burns Supper circuit can well imagine Rabbie behind the plough. Currie does not have to imagine. He has been between the stilts and smelt the rich earth folding beneath the blade. Literary brains may appraise the bard's words: Currie loves them and lives them:

> Nae treasures nor pleasures
> Could make us happy lang;
> The heart ay's the part ay
> That makes us right or wrang.

On one occasion, at a Burns Supper in the shadow of his own Drumadoon, James broke his golden rule and was overtly political. It was spontaneous. Burns would not have stood by idly and watched the heart being torn out of Scotia. Currie spoke of shipyards and steelworks closing; small firms folding; and nothing being done to create fresh jobs. 'Scotland is getting a raw deal. It's time that was said and it's time something was done about it.'

> If I'm design'd yon lordling's slave –
> By Nature's law design'd –
> Why was an independent wish
> E're planted in my mind?
> If not, why am I subject to
> His cruelty, or scorn?
> Or why has man the will and pow'r
> To make his fellow mourn?

In his latter years, James Currie became more outspoken about his political views. He was a socialist, and regarded himself as such rather than a member of a political party. He believed that the strong should help the weak, indeed his ministry was based on that. His answer to criticism that members of the Church should not become involved in politics was simple: if politics was about people and their welfare then that *was* the work of the Church. The two were inextricably linked.

If Burns had not written the line 'A man's a man for a' that', then Currie might have. Certainly, both were appalled by man's inhumanity to man, and both had a waspish sense of humour, frequently directed at themselves. The minister told the tale of the time when a man got up and wandered off in the middle of one of his sermons. The man's wife explained later: 'It's all right, Mr Currie, he walks in his sleep.'

James told the Arran Burns Supper that he had been visiting an old folks' home where the television set had packed up. Mrs McGlumpher, to break the boredom, decided to streak through the gardens. Two of the residents caught a flash of her. 'Whit was that?' one asked. 'It was auld McGlumpher,' the other explained. 'An' whit was she wearin'? 'I don't know, but it was too big fur her.'

This was one of Currie's 'dirty stories'. It was told to him by his granddaughter, Irene, then aged ten.

Then there was the woman in Pollok who was ashamed because her budgie kept saying, 'Whoopie, I'm a good time girl.' Currie said he would put matters right. His budgie was a reverent fellow, always on its knees praying. He would take the 'good time girl' home and let his budgie teach her a lesson. As he walked in the door, there was a loud cry of 'Whoopie, I'm a good time girl.' His own budgie got down on its knees and said, 'Thank you, my prayers have been answered!'

152

Another Pollok woman told him that she had had a disturbing dream. She was in heaven, with a piece of chalk, writing down all her sins. 'And you were in the dream, Mr Currie.' He asked, 'Was I in heaven?' She replied, 'No, you were on your way back down for another piece of chalk.'

Burns too, would have needed a fair supply of chalk. But Currie had no doubt that he was in heaven. That woman in Pollok told the minister that there were many things about Burns's life that she did not like. There were things she would not like her sons to emulate, but Rabbie created some of the best poems ever written and gave the world its finest love songs. A man without a soul could not have done that, and only a man without a soul would not find forgiveness.

Tens of thousands went to listen to Currie on Burns. After almost every speech, he would look for the people who went to talk to him. The ones holding back at a table, or standing in a corner. Those were the people who wanted to hear from the minister, the people who did not go to church but wanted the advice of the churchman. They were the recruits in his widespread ministry, the ones who responded when he took his broad church to the people.

After speaking at a Burns Supper in the North of Scotland, 'where some ministers are so strict that Jesus would find it difficult to get into their kirks,' James was offering guidance and advice after 1.00 am. He still had a four-hour drive home, and a funeral service to conduct at 10.00 am. Such incidents were not uncommon.

CHAPTER FIFTEEN

Rangers

Glasgow Rangers! Glasgow Rangers!
He'll support you ever more,
Ever more,
He'll support you ever more!

James Currie's love of Glasgow Rangers Football Club, fervent when he was a child, grew stronger as he grew older. It was a reciprocal affair, with club officials, players, and members of the supporters' federation staying true to Currie to the last. But it was a relationship which won him as many enemies as it did friends. This hurt him, but did not diminish his passion. And it was a passion.

The boy at Drumadoon would race to the greenkeeper's house on Saturday evenings to hear the football scores. It was 'a hop and a skip back when Rangers won, a hundred-mile trudge when they lost.' One thing about Keil College upset him. Its colours were green. 'Green, imagine that, me in green – I think you could really make something of that – the Rangers boys would love it.'

One of his proudest boasts was that pictures of former managers Jock Wallace and John Greig shared a wall at the supporters' club while his photograph had one to itself. The honourary season ticket which he had received every year since his Pollok days, was a treasured possession. Photographs taken with players adorned the walls of the manse.

How did he regard the association with a club castigated in the past for alleged sectarianism and reluctance to sign Roman Catholics.

He said, 'I'm a fan, Rangers daft, and proud of it. It's a great club, run by fine men. And so are the leaders of the supporters' federation. They're good men. I'm proud to be associated with them.' As in all aspects of his life 'it all happened by accident. I never looked for any of it – but I welcomed it.'

Glasgow Rangers are one of the best supported clubs in Britain. Attendances at Ibrox Stadium are in excess of 40 000 with major games assured of a 44 000 sell-out. The club, managed by Graeme

Proud pose in the trophy room.

Souness, former captain of the Scottish international team, has paid more than six million to sign players over the past two years. Thousands have found their way back to Ibrox to bask in the glamour and success brought by this adventurous policy. Their support might have been more valuable some years back when the club was going through a lean spell. James Currie was not a fair weather fan. He followed the club through thick and thin, giving vocal support not only at matches but in other, more contentious issues.

Many thousands of Rangers supporters are notorious for their anti-Roman Catholic chants. It must also be stated that similar numbers who follow rivals Celtic err on the other side. However, at the time of writing, there is one fundamental difference between the teams. The green and white hoops of Celtic have been worn by many Protestants. The number of Roman Catholics who have donned the light blue of Rangers can be counted on the fingers of one hand. This had done little to stifle the anti-Catholic chants from the follow-follow brigade.

A friend of mine, who is a sports journalist, once asked Jock Stein when he was manager of Celtic which youngster he would sign if all things were equal and one lad was RC and the other Protestant. Without hesitation, Stein replied: 'The Protestant – because I know Rangers wouldn't sign the Catholic.'

Rangers, despite public statements that they are equal opportunities employers, have yet to play a Roman Catholic in the first team. In the mid 1970s, there was a concerted campaign in the media suggesting that this apparent policy should be dropped. Willie Waddell, the club's general manager, called a press conference and stated that the club neither condoned nor supported sectarianism.

He said: 'We are determined to end Rangers image as a sectarian club. Rangers Football Club divorces themselves completely from religious and sectarian bias in every respect on the field of play and on the terracings. No religious barriers will be put up by this club regarding the signing of players. As far as humanly possible every measure will be taken to remove spectators from Ibrox who do not acept this policy.'

Mr Waddell maintained, however, that there had not been a policy of excluding Roman Catholic players. He said that the fact that only a handful of Catholics had been signed by the club in more than a hundred years was, as far as he knew, 'coincidence'.

Rangers would sign a Roman Catholic players when a suitable one became available. Some months later, when the club had failed to find 'a suitable player', the press questioned the sincerity of the statement.

The Ibrox hierarchy reiterated its intention, but declined to elaborate or answer further questions. It takes two to tangle, and it was at this stage that James Currie entered the fray. He had a letter published in *The Glasgow Herald* criticising the media's 'mischievous harassment' of the club. A champion had stepped forward.

Currie accepted a challenge to appear on a live television sports programme to discuss the issue. He made it clear on the air that he held no position in the club and could not speak for the views of the directors. He knew that he would get a rough ride, but it is perhaps an indication of innocence that he felt he was tricked into discussing the 'continuing policy of Rangers' sectarianism.'

Was this one occasion when he wished that he had been able to say 'No', to a challenge?

'Oh no, definitely not,' he said. 'I was upset by the criticism but I felt I had to stand up for the club. Nobody else was doing it, and the press was kicking the Rangers when they were down. The directors had said they would sign a Roman Catholic. Why couldn't the journalists just leave them alone to get on with their business? The media only made matters more difficult. They were stirring up a storm in a teacup.'

Currie found himself tossed into the centre of that storm and branded by some as a bigot. And this 'bigot', remember, is the man who had been rebuked by the Church of Scotland's hierarchy for ushering Roman Catholics into his kirk, baptising their children, and taking part in RC wedding services. He had the courage to support the club he loved when the going got tough. When his team were the underdogs he backed them as best he knew how. Currie was always a man for the underdog.

What were his views? Did he want to see Rangers sign Roman Catholics?

He said: 'On that programme I said that we should sign Frank McGarvey, who was a Celtic stalwart at the time. He's also a Roman Catholic. But I hate labels. Protestant, Catholic, Hindu, Moslem – Burns said "a man's a man for a' that" – and his religion or the colour of his skin doesn't matter one little bit. It's never mattered to me.'

'But what the journalists didn't ask, and what they should have been asking, was whether Frank McGarvey would *want* to play for Rangers. It's difficult, you know. Children grow up with their team. Any good Catholic boy wants to play for Celtic, doesn't he? The same as a Protestant boy wants to play for Rangers. It's all very well criticising, but it's not as easy as that.'

A Roman Catholic who pulled on the club's blue jersey would have to be a special man. Rangers' first RC would be under a great deal of pressure, not just on the park but in his everyday life. How would his children be treated at a Catholic school? It was not just the man who would be going to Ibrox, but his family as well.

'But I'd like to see them sign Paul McStay from Celtic. By jings I would. He's a Rangers type.'

He's also a Roman Catholic.

Currie used his love for Rangers throughout his ministry. Jim Martin uttered his 'most important words' at James's induction at Renton – 'I must tell you . . . he is a Rangers supporter.' Ian McColl, a half-back with the club in the 1950s, opened a fête in the manse gardens at Millburn. George Brown, who also played with Rangers in the 1950s and was a director of the club in the 1960s, was a senior teacher at a school which Currie visited every Monday morning. One day, when the conversation turned to football, James said that he'd often applauded Brown from the terraces.

'I'll have to see about getting you a season ticket,' the teacher said.

Later that week, the director delivered the season ticket to the manse and that was a major step in the minister's deep involvement with the club.

Currie's clerical collar became a familiar sight in the main stand at Ibrox Stadium. The man who believed in taking the Church to the people could hardly have chosen a bigger stage. And, as at Renton, the opportunity arose because he was simply being himself. He got to know the people at the club, from the directors to the doorman and the blokes who swept the terraces. He spoke to folk and they began to realise they could talk to him. Talk about Rangers, and, as bonds of trust were formed, talk about their own problems.

Lex McLean, the Glasgow comedian, was Rangers daft. He was due to compere a concert for the supporters' federation but had to call off through illness. James was invited to take his place and give a speech.

'I was delighted,' he said. 'A minister asked to go to an occasion like that! They realised that the Church was not all doom and gloom but was a way of life with a place for fun and enjoyment. I was well received and they enjoyed my stories. So much so that I came in for some abuse behind the scenes from the comedian on the bill. He said that it wasn't me but my clerical collar that was getting the laughs. He gave me quite a hard time.'

This was not the only occasion when Currie's collar was attacked by a comedian. James spoke at a function at the Royal Albert Hall and had the audience in stitches. 'I think that night saw the greatest compliment I was ever paid. A professional entertainer said I turned the Royal Albert into a village hall, and that's just what it was like – a ceilidh round the fire.' The comedian, Jimmy Tarbuck, did not have the same success or rapport with the audience. He realised that Currie was the crowd's darling, and attempted to move in on this wavelength.

James said, 'But he took the wrong line. He said on stage 'It's his bloody collar you're laughing at. And that fell flat. In fairness, he was wise enough to realise his mistake and changed tack. He told clean stories, good stories, and was well received.'

Later, on Michael Parkinson's chat show, Tarbuck was asked who made him laugh. Immediately he spoke about 'the vicar at the Royal Albert Hall.'

The whole of Scotland was stunned in January 1972, by the Ibrox Disaster. Sixty-six people died and many more were seriously injured when part of the terracing collapsed as a huge crowd was leaving the stadium after a match against Celtic.

The Currie family was on Arran. James had just returned to the manse after conducting a wedding service when the telephone rang. It was a club official. He did not know the magnitude of the disaster, but he wanted James to come to the ground to minister to the injured. Currie lifted his Bible and ran the half-mile from the manse to the stadium. On the way, he was passed by a fleet of police cars, ambulances and fire engines.

The scene outside the ground was one of total confusion. Thousands were making their way home, oblivious to the disaster. Others, alerted by the wail of sirens and an early radio broadcast that four people had been injured, were attempting to return to the stadium. Then a deathly hush fell on the area. It was reminiscent of the torpedo factory at Alexandria after the explosion '. . . if Currie's no here he's on his way.'

A Rangers fan recognised the minister and shouted to his friends to clear a path. The word spread and the fans parted like the Red Sea. The main gates at Ibrox were guarded by stewards under strict instructions to allow admission only to members of the emergency services. They ushered the minister in.

James Currie would not dwell on the scenes in Ibrox Stadium. He said prayers over the bodies that were laid row after row in front of the main stand. Helped to tend to the injured. Tried to comfort relatives. 'I did what I could.'

He went to the Southern General Hospital, then to the Victoria Infirmary, then back to Ibrox to say a prayer with the club officials. Then he went back to the hospitals.

'What a terrible tragedy,' he said. 'So many lives, and so many of them young lives . . .'

In 1976, Currie's association with the club seemed ready to yield a large dividend. He received a letter from Willie Waddell congratulating him on a recent BBC Television Songs of Praise broadcast from Dunlop. Rangers had arranged to play Motherwell on Boxing Day, a Sunday, would James like to conduct carol singing at Ibrox? He accepted with enthusiasm.

'What a wonderful evangelical opportunity,' he said. 'I always talk about taking the Church to the people: here were the people bringing the Church to themselves. And what church could get 40000 people singing carols?'

He set about co-ordinating the arrangements. Two choirs were contacted and agreed to come along. Two bands – from Govan and Motherwell – were happy to play, and a conductor was appointed. Currie would be master of ceremonies.

But his 'wonderful evangelical opportunity' was thwarted by Glasgow Presbytery. A fellow minister, from Ibrox, raised objections. It was argued that Currie was being used as the thin edge of the wedge to gain respectability for Sunday football. The media fastened on to the row. The club said it was 'a one-off occasion', and declared its opposition to matches being played on a regular basis on Sundays. A regional councillor said that the disruption would upset many local people and transport facilities. Folk would have difficulty, for example, visiting relatives in the Southern General Hospital. Through it all, Currie remained silent but unrepentant. He saw the opportunity as the very essence of his particular style of preaching. Others could threaten hellfire and eternal damnation: his ministry was about living and a happier, better way of life. He knew that for many of the 40000 crowd participating in the carol singing it would be their only act of worship that year. And he saw it as worship. However, on this occasion, as on many others, this simple philosophy backfired on him.

The controversy continued and there seemed to be no way out. Then Willie Waddell resolved the impasse.

James said, 'He was concerned about the way I was being treated and decided to resolve the matter by withdrawing the invitation to me and cancelling the carol service. I know he did it with my interests at heart, and I appreciate that and respect him for it, but I wish we had gone ahead. The carol singing could have become a regular feature and would have opened so many doors.'

James Currie was a great admirer of Jock Wallace, the former Rangers' manager. The minister used one of the manager's favourite words to sum him up, 'Character, now there's a man with real character.'

Wallace instilled the importance of this quality into his players: it was not a substitute for skill, rather a necessary complement in a man for all seasons – a winner. It was a passionate love for Glasgow Rangers Football Club that brought the two men together, but their relationship transcended that, and a friendship was born out of a respect for the other's industry and single-minded pursuit of his goal. .

They used different words to define 'character'. Wallace saw it as the ability 'to overcome a knock-back. To be able to fight back and succeed. I signed players who'd had rebuffs in life but came back and fought again.'

Currie said it was a combination of dignity, integrity and perseverance.

'I'd agree with all that,' Jock said when we spoke in his Bothwell home a year after James's death. 'I'd never thought of it that way. I'm an uneducated man. James could put into words what I felt. Now he *had* character. He was with Rangers in the bad days as well as the good days. I was happy to see him coming about the club on a day-to-day basis. He was always willing to offer his services for weddings, funerals and the like. He was a Churchman first and, as far as I'm concerned, the Rangers came a close second. I never saw him without his collar on. He always wore it. He was a man of the cloth and he carried that dignity with him. We had many a happy time together, and Peggy too. I respected him. I'll tell you this – I really loved James.'

This is not a word the former soldier in the King's Own Scottish Borderers uses lightly. It is sincere. He wants to know how Peggy is keeping. Last time he saw her she was 'looking great, and I take some consolation out of that, but she looked lonely. But what can you do . . . it's memories that keep you going.'

Jock Wallace had no time for those who criticised James Currie's love of Rangers. Folk had a right to a different allegiance, but, he said, James's association with the club was open, honest, and sincere.

He sat in Currie's kirk on Sunday morning when he was godfather to a child of Jock Dalziel, a friend from his days in the Army in the jungles of Malaya. 'And James said from the pulpit, "Who's here today but Jock Wallace, the manager of Glasgow Rangers – now there's a man." And I had a big red face!'

Jock was in Spain, managing Seville, when James died. 'I really felt it bad when I heard about James's death. He really believed in what he was doing. He did it with humanity, humility and sincerity. I loved the man – absolutely loved the man – and Peggy too. They were a twosome who got on with each other – like me and Daph – and the fact that he was a Rangers fanatic was purely incidental, but it helped to put the gloss on our friendship.'

Daphne Wallace echoed her husband's sentiments. She was very fond of James, 'a super bloke'. She met him through the club, but got to know him as a minister when she spent almost three months in hospital in 1978 with a serious illness.

'James was very nice,' she said. 'He came in the afternoons when there weren't many visitors and just chatted. He made a point of visiting others – he was very busy, always rushing around because he had that much to do – but once he'd sat down on the edge of the bed he always made the time to talk. He was very supportive, and good at encouraging you to talk. But he never said much about himself.'

What was the main topic of conversation?

'Oh, it was Rangers. What Rangers should have done and what they shouldn't have done.'

This is a subject with which Daphne Wallace is well acquainted.

Her illness came at a particularly trying time for the family. Jock had left Rangers and taken over at Leicester, a team struggling in the second division. Because of the nature of the illness, their two children, then aged fifteen and sixteen, were not allowed into hospital to see her. The demands of Jock's new job meant that he could only drive up at weekends, returning to Leicester to supervise training on Monday mornings. This was a time, according to James, when Jock showed his true character.

The minister said: 'There was a man, husband and breadwinner, who was not sure where his responsibility lay. He had committed himself to help a team and then his wife became seriously ill. There was Daph in hospital and Jock hundreds of miles away living in a hotel. But he stuck to it. A time like that would have broken a lesser man.'

Did Jock ask James to visit Daph?

Wallace, 'No. I knew that I'd just have to mention it to him though.'

He pauses, thinking back, and then comes a statement in character: 'How can you ask a man to do what you can't do yourself? But when Daph told me James had been in to see her it was just great. I got solace out of that. I'll never forget it.'

Any player who survived the strenuous routine Jock Wallace put them through on the sand dunes of Gullane, which became known as Murder Hill, will tell you that he is a hard task-master. He gave his all, and expected no less in return. He admired Currie's industry.

'He worked hard. He went out among the people. He was all for the people. He could talk to them and they'd listen. He'd talk about Rangers and Celtic. He talked about life and he understood what it was all about. He believed emphatically in what he was doing and it came across. He had no pretentions. He was a man of the people – and I'd like to think I'm a man of the people.'

He's quiet for a bit. Perhaps he's not going to tell me what he's thinking. Then he says: 'There wasn't a church big enough for James. His church was always full. I listened to him – deep, sincere, honest and humble.'

He pauses again. 'It's crazy the things you think about. Do you know the biggest tribute I could pay James Currie? They should have gone to Texas and got him a prairie. And he'd have filled that! I can see him there, preaching the Gospel, full of passion and belief and hard work. He was a good, working man and a good guy. He believed in what he was doing, as I believed in what I was doing. I told him: 'You've made some cowboys happy, boy.' I'll tell you this. He made one cowboy happy – he made me happy.

'James reached the top. He worked hard to fill his church and he kept it that way. He made mistakes and corrected them. That's life. Who's perfect? We were the same – we believed in what we were doing. I worked for Rangers and he worked for God. It's as simple as that.'

James Currie was regarded as chaplain to the Rangers' Supporters Federation, and hence, by unspoken agreement, to the club itself. He conducted the wedding service for Derek Parlane, centre forward for Rangers and Scotland, and spoke at Gordon Smith's wedding reception 'because his minister didn't believe in going to receptions. I think that's just plain daft. What better time is there to meet people than when they're happy? And what better time is there to let them know that the kirk can laugh too?'

As always for a minister there were sad responsibilities too. He

163

conducted the funeral service of Bobby McKean, a talented player who had yet to reach the peak of his career.

His work with Rangers supporters would take a book in itself to chronicle, but that is the last word on his mission to take the Church to the people. Many of them came to the Church. It is true that a large proportion did not linger, but when they needed help the doors were open. Perhaps James Currie's association with Glasgow Rangers best describes his style of ministry and how he, and others, looked upon it. Currie's critics point to his love of the club and brand him a bigot. Those who believe that the minister, and the Church as a whole, should cater for the needs of the ordinary man, have a fuller understanding of what he was attempting to do.

He was a supporter of Rangers: a servant of God.

CHAPTER SIXTEEN

Dunlop

James Currie had been dead for a year when the vacancy committee appointed by officers of Laigh Kirk, Dunlop, chose a replacement minister.

James did not want to go to Dunlop. This is not an insult to the congregation there or to the kirk itself. The simple fact is that despite the many frustrations and problems which beset him at Pollok he was in love with the place and the people. The names of St James and James Currie had become almost synonymous. However, as the congregation of St James's became healthier, the health of the minister deteriorated. Currie the shy man hated change. Despite his success, it was as if he did not have the confidence to move. James Mason had told him to go to Renton; Lord MacLeod of Fuinary told him to 'go through the door in faith' to Pollok; and Dr McGregor told him to go to Dunlop.

The Ayrshire village was a complete contrast to the bustling housing scheme in Glasgow. Its congregation was about a tenth the size of that in Pollok: its demands, therefore, were reduced proportionately. Currie's family and friends were delighted when he made the move, and happier still when it appeared that he had accepted that he could not continue to work sixteen hours a day, every day. Not everyone in the kirk was happy with the choice of minister. Currie's name, and his political views, preceded him and were not to the liking of some of the more well-to-do in the congregation. When they met the man, they were won over.

It will come as no surprise as to what Currie did during his first few weeks at Dunlop. He visited the sick, the poor, and those in need of assistance. He had a lot in common with the people of his new parish, perhaps more so than he had with the folk of Pollok. Dunlop is a village, a close-knit community not unlike that of Blackwaterfoot. It is a farming village, inhabited by hard-working, good-living people. It did not take him long to settle in, to get to know his parish, and get to work on his 'broad church'. The workload of Laigh Kirk was, indeed, much lighter than that of St James. Currie had, reluctantly, complied

with doctor's orders to go to Ayrshire. He had not promised to go into 'semi-retirement'.

He gave the parish at least eight hours work a day, but that left eight hours of his working day. These rapidly became filled with extra-curricular Currie activities. Burns, fiddlers' rallies, attending functions to speak on a variety of topics – and wearing his clerical collar at every one. He seized the opportunity to expand his broad church: to take the church to the people. This took him all over Scotland and to a variety of countries. He drove 30 000 miles a year.

Some of the people on the periphery of Currie's work remarked that Drumadoon must be the ideal spot for rest and recuperation. Many envied the minister who could stroll in the rolling hills lording it over the Mull of Kintyre, heather tugging at his tweeds, his only task to throw a stone for a sheep dog to collect. The gentle lapping of the waves a calming reassurance that life goes on, life goes on . . . not inexorablably but as part of the Great Plan.

Currie's closest companions spent their holidays at Drumadoon. They returned home leaner, fitter and with a better appreciation of

Ron Vavasour

After the wedding of Calum and Christie Kennedy.

the demands of their own jobs and routine. James offered 'working holidays'. On one occasion cement had to be laid as a floor for a new shed. Parish duties had put the starting time back by four hours and light was failing when James, Peggy, Iain, Charles and Laura Kennedy began the task. The women fed a cement mixer while father and sons, regularly exchanging stern criticism of each other, carted and spread and levelled the mixture. There was no electricity supply in the shed, so when a thick mist descended with the darkness there was a move to down tools. Currie the socialist imposed a compromise and suspended a powerful torch from the roof. When Charles complained that he could not see what he was doing his father tied torches to the shovels with baler twine! Around 11.00 pm, against all odds, the task was completed and the team stepped back to admire the work. Well, almost all of the team stepped back. The minister stumbled, arms flailing, and would have regained his balance but for the ample girth which tugged him forward and down. He made a big impression on the freshly-laid cement. Exit workmates, stage left, laughing all the way. Currie saw the funny side – eventually. The incident was used time and again in the minister's addresses.

Humour played a large part in his life. In Argyle Street with friends he saw the awesome, imposing figure of a dignitary from the Roman Catholic Church clad from head to toe in black, clerical robes. The crowd parted before him as he marched along purposefully. An assistant, laden with parcels, followed in the man's wake. When one of James's friends asked who it was, Currie replied, 'The valet of the shadow of death.'

Currie feared no ill when walking in that valley, and he reassured others. One three-year-old who recently saw his mother crying asked what was wrong. She said she had been thinking about the boy's grandfather who had died. 'It's all right mum,' the boy said. 'Granddad's playing football with Mr Currie in heaven.' Is there a better explanation?

James Currie's church was broad in all respects. His idea of the ministry was not just to tend to spiritual needs, he wanted it to go further and embrace day-to-day problems which caused his parishioners concern. He helped people to face up to debts and criminal offences, taking on a role similar to that of today's social worker, and early in his career he investigated alternative means of treating illness. He had faith in the healing ministry – the laying on hands to cure or alleviate sickness. Clarence Finlayson, who was also a believer in this, was responsible for James meeting a remarkable man, the Revd Cameron Peddie, of Hutchestown Church in the Gorbals.

Peddie had been in the Victoria Infirmary, Glasgow, for an operation when he befriended a 30-year-old man who was sent home to die. Doctors could do no more for him. The minister, however, believed that through the Lord's commission, Preach the gospel, heal the sick, he should be able to cure an incurable disease.

Peddie set aside a room in his house as a sanctuary for prayer and meditation to prepare himself for his chosen work. He devoted an hour a day to this task. He prepared himself for five years before he was sent a sign that he was the instrument of extraordinary powers.

At noon on 17 May 1947, at the age of sixty and exactly thirty years after his ordination, Cameron Peddie was alone in his house peeling potatoes. In a book called *The Forgotten Talent*, he writes that as he stood at his kitchen sink he 'suddenly felt gripped by a strange benevolent power that filled me with an unspeakable sense of happiness . . . joy filled my heart and overflowed in tears . . . I had reached the home of ultimate truth and all things were clear and plain.' Three months later he asked God for another sign to confirm his belief in his new powers. He wrote, 'I saw something very strange. My hand grew smaller, and became all bruised, as if it had been hammered. Then down from the roots of the first two fingers and between them, a large nail appeared driven in to the very head; from it blood trickled down the lines on the palm and round the wrist. I cannot say how long the vision lasted for time did not exist for me.'

In May 1948, Peddie conducted his first healing service. A friend had been seriously ill with a heart condition, rheumatism and deafness in one ear. After he laid hands on the woman her heart pain disappeared, as did her other ailments. The success was not recorded, although the woman was the wife of a journalist, because the minister wanted no publicity. His second case was a cancer sufferer who had been sent home from hospital to die, probably within a matter of weeks. Cameron Peddie laid hands on her and the pain disappeared. A day after the healing service she was able to get out of bed. The woman lived for a year in comparative comfort.

The ailments which Peddie treated with success range from osteoarthritis to corns and bunions. Inevitably, word spread about his powers and, somewhat reluctantly, he bowed to the wishes of fellow ministers and held a public healing service at St James's Church in Pollok.

When James Currie's father was in hospital dying Cameron Peddie visited him. Drumadoon's kidneys had failed, and a painful death was imminent. Peddie laid hands on the old farmer and almost immediately the man was calmed. The pain seemed to disappear, and Drumadoon fell into a deep sleep and passed away peacefully. James said, 'It gave me tremendous comfort to know that my father's last hours were painless and dignified.'

'You never know when you'll meet people who'll be a major influence in your life. You never know the man or woman, and you never know the minute.'

James Currie said words to this effect time and again. One such man is John Mason MBE, a solicitor in Troon, and a highly-respected musician and composer. This man's influence on the minister was considerable, but his contribution after James's death will ensure that Currie's name endures and, more importantly, that his life's work continues.

Their paths crossed shortly after James took over at Laigh Kirk. The Kilmarnock Caledonia Strathspey and Reel Society had put on a concert at St James's and its leaders had been so impressed by Currie's talent as master of ceremonies that they asked him to compere their annual concert at the Grand Hall in Kilmarnock. John Mason was one of the fiddlers in the orchestra who got added enjoyment from performing with the minister who was, by this time, earning a reputation as an entertainer.

John Mason's first love was music, but he was to go on to study law. If Currie was torn between the plough and the pulpit this young man faced the dilemma of choosing between legal briefs and musical notes, 'My father asked me if I'd ever heard of a full-time musician who was a part-time lawyer, so my choice of career was evident.' Like James, however, he succeeded in achieving both ambitions and, in 1972, helped to establish the Ayr and Prestwick Strathspey and Reel Society (The Strings of Scotland). Many of the orchestra's performances, sometimes two a week, were for charity, and James was delighted when he was asked to act as compere. In October the following year, a big fiddlers' rally organised as part of the Mod at Dam Park in Ayr was televised live and, again, the minister was centre stage. The event was greeted with great enthusiasm and a record was released – the first ever – of massed fiddle playing. Some of those early performances were before an audience of twenty or thirty, in a church hall or old folks' home, but they were to lead to sell-out shows for more than 6000 people at the Royal Albert Hall in London.

As the reputation of the orchestra spread, John Mason's demanding standards and ambitions increased. He wrote music, which is widely acclaimed, and he wanted it to be performed by the best. An invitation was sent out to all the Strathspey and Reel societies to send their two best players to audition for Mason's dream – and, in 1982, the Scottish Fiddle Orchestra was born. It performs before sell-out audiences at the Caird Hall in Dundee; the City Hall, Glasgow; Music Hall, Aberdeen; the Usher Hall of Edinburgh as well as the Royal Albert Hall in London.

'James never failed to turn up for a performance,' John Mason said. 'He was a brilliant link man and a natural comedian. He could handle 6000 people in the Royal Albert or twenty-five folk in a wee village hall. The size of the audience did not matter to him. In fact, he could be better with the twenty-five, and any performer will tell you how difficult that task is.

'Our performances at the Royal Albert Hall were recorded. James insisted that we included waltzes in the programme, and that was part of his own performance.'

As the first bar of the waltz floated across the hall Currie would begin the routine: 'Now, some lucky girl is going to dance with me and I've got two left feet!'

Then he would march to the front of the stage, usually raised five feet above the audience and ask to be helped down. He would pretend to overstretch, arms whirling in mock panic. Elderly ladies in the front rows would catch their breath as strong men raced to catch the minister. Two members of the orchestra lowered him as the music got into full swing.

'Every time I saw him hovering on the edge of the stage I thought he was going to collapse,' Mason said. 'And in that voice he'd be pleading, 'Can you help me down, please.'

'He danced at every concert. In the recordings, the music at the beginning of each waltz is barely audible because of the applause. That marks James being helped down off the stage. Then he would switch partners and the applause would start again. He would ruin the recording with this. And all the time he'd be roaring with laughter.'

John Mason stops and thinks back. His soft, Orcadian voice falls even lower as he says: 'It's a nice memory.'

The two men had a deep respect and affection for each other. The partnership actually brought about what James described as 'the greatest tribute ever paid to me. I was told that I brought a full house at the Royal Albert Hall down to a ceilidh. Isn't that great? Isn't that what it's all about?'

John Mason praised Currie the comedian. 'He was a supreme

entertainer. He knew exactly how to treat his audience. He had two or three very good jokes. They might have been old, but they were very good and he could tell them. I'd heard them umpteen times and I still laughed. He would use these jokes to test the water and, depending on how his audience reacted, he would tailor his act to suit. He was never smutty, but he could be risqué, and his method of his delivery was perfect.'

James got a buzz from applause. Laughter is the comedian's currency and he was not one to short-change his audience. His timing of a punchline was superb, but his appreciation of deadlines, so vital in the smooth running of a show, left much to be desired. This is fine in the village hall where the public get more than their money's worth, but at the Royal Albert, where severe financial penalties can be imposed if a performance over-runs by ten minutes, it can be a costly business.

Following a concert at the Royal Albert Hall, Mason said, 'We'd been over-running and it was proving expensive, so I hammered in the concert to finish at 10.20 pm. I thought we'd made it. There was plenty of time for James's vote of thanks, but after he'd delivered it he started to tell stories. I nearly died! Then he thanked the hall keepers, the folk who sold the programmes – everybody but the painters. They were stars, he said, give them a big hand. And after finishing the performance well in time we did over-run. Fortunately, they didn't charge us, but I made it plain to James that I was angry. he said on many occasions that he was sorry that he'd hurt me and that he didn't mean to. When he got started he just couldn't stop.'

The apology was sincere. James had told me about the incident: 'I lost track of time and got carried away, but it's nice to thank the people like the programme sellers. They're every bit as important, you know.'

John Mason has not run an orchestra of 120 musicians without learning a thing or two abut the eggshell temperament of the performer, but he said: 'James was the most easily injured man I've ever met. He got upset if someone – just one out of 6000 – didn't laugh. He'd look at them from the stage and say, 'What's wrong, do you not think that's funny?' That one person could spoil the whole evening for him. But he was a great, giving man. A tremendous, giving man. After a performance at the Albert Hall, when we were all high and tired, he would leave quickly to catch the last train home to begin his real work in the pulpit on Sunday morning. Our job was done, but his was just beginning. If we were over-running he would ask if anybody in the audience could give him a lift to the station. In the Royal Albert, cadging a lift from the stage! And he got it. But that's just the way he was. Friends give you a lift in their car and James Currie was among friends. That was a large part of his success. Every member of the audience regarded him as a friend. He was the link between the orchestra and the audience – and what a superb link. He barely covered his costs. He never asked for anything.'

As with Burns Suppers, after-dinner speeches or any public appearance, James Currie wore his clerical collar at fiddlers' rallies. Had John Mason seen people waiting to speak to the minister rather than the performer?

'Do you know, I was never conscious of that. It never struck me. There were always people around him, dozens of them, but until Peggy explained it after James had died I never considered that possibility.'

The performer's public persona was high-profile; confidences shared with the minister were private.

At the time, John Mason did not recognise Currie's broad church in operation, but it touched him. He knew the preacher behind the punchlines. At James's funeral he was approached by Robert Innes, head of extra-mural studies at Stirling University, and asked if he would help to ensure the continuation of the minister's work through the foundation of a trust fund.

'It was a great idea and I agreed immediately,' he said.

The trustees of the James Currie Memorial Trust have been working quietly raising capital. It is based at Airthrey Castle, The University, Stirling, and its members cover a cross-section of society. They include Jack Bowman, Chief Constable of Tayside; Anne Clarke, a senior member of the National Association of Carers; Dr Gerry Crean, a world authority on gastroenterology; singer Mary Sandeman; Robert Kernohan, editor of the Kirk's magazine *Life and Work;* Ian Collie, director of education for Central Region; Margaret Bell, retired Matron of the Southern General Hospital in Glasgow; Robbie Shepherd, broadcasting personality; Reesa McGinn, a teacher; and James Mackay, editor of the *Burnsian*. Their aim is laudable.

John Mason said, 'We want to provide cash to help the ordinary man, woman and child – those described by James as the salt of the earth. James was comfortable in front of an audience of 6000, but his main role, his gut feeling if you like, was for ordinary men. The ones who tugged at his heart strings. He helped them when he was alive and our ambition is to continue to help them, in James's name, after his death. We haven't heard of a comparable trust in Scotland.'

Mason was well aware of Currie's popularity. 'At the end of a show, or at the interval, he'd be mobbed by people. It was pandemonium, and he'd be handling out pamphlets for the next rally, or brochures on his visits to the Holy Land, or arranging to speak at a Burns Supper. He could do so many things at once.

'I remember one day when my wife, Hilary, and I called at the manse to discuss arrangements for a rally. Two women were visiting Peggy. James was sitting in a big leather chair, conducting a conversation with them, watching a football match on television and listening to a rugby international on radio. As we were talking about the rally, suddenly he turned to Hilary and said, 'You're a farmer's daughter, would you like to see my cattle?' So we were rushed into his car and driven at high speed to The Glebe. As he ran over the field to bring the cattle to the gates, he shouted to me to listen to the car radio and keep track of the scores. No sooner had he rounded up the cattle than he was back in the car, back to the manse and the telly and radio. He picked up the conversation with Peggy's friends, discussed our family with Hilary, spoke to Peggy about what we'd all have for supper, tried to conduct a conversation with me about the concert – and, in between times, he was whistling Cock o' the North! It was frightening. I came out of there trembling at the sight of all this energy. *I* was tired.

'But I never found that doing shows with him. He was tremendously supportive. A big show could drain me of energy and James would just take over. I'd no doubts about his abilities. He would just come on and bolster the show. On one occasion when I was to introduce the next singer I just blacked out mentally. I don't know what was wrong. I asked James to do it and he strolled on to the stage and performed as if it had been rehearsed. He was never far from the stage door . . . always there if I needed him. And the audience loved him. He would introduce me as "that great friend, gifted man of music, John Johann Sebastian Mason." He was the best PR man I ever had.'

Currie was widely criticised for the amount of time he spent in connection with the world of entertainment. He said that his parish did not suffer, 'I was always there when I was needed. I never, never put off parish work to appear at anything but I cancelled many, many bookings to look after my parishioners.' His involvement with the fiddlers' rallies brought about one particular occasion where his broad church crossed religious divides.

Dan Larkin, from Garrykennedy, County Tipperary, is one of the fiddlers in John Mason's orchestra. His wife, Joan, accompanied him to a performance in Edinburgh. On the Sunday morning, John Mason asked if they wanted to go to church. They replied that they did, and would like to hear James preach. Dan and Joan are Roman Catholic. John explained that James was a minister in the Church of Scotland. That did not matter to the Irish couple. They wanted to hear James preach. They went to Laigh Kirk and received a warm welcome. 'The sermon was superb, I'll never forget it,' John Mason said. 'And as we left the church Dan said, 'If we had priests like that across the water there wouldn't be the trouble there is today'.

The Scottish Fiddle Orchestra dedicated the proceeds from a series of performances to the James Currie Memorial Trust. The highlights were tunes John composed and dedicated to James, *The Arran Shepherd, The Drumadoon Reel, John Mason's Compliments to the Revd James Currie*, and an overture entitled *The Friend of Man*.

Mason said, 'When attempting to encompass in our national music a suitable tribute to the memory of James, I experienced a great difficulty in determining a suitable title. Elsie Smith, of Troon, directed me to the verses written by Robert Burns on the death of his own father and nowhere could one have found more apt references for the overture title. James was indeed 'The Friend of Man'. His active interest so broad, his faith so strong, his sheer exuberance and energy affected and inspired everyone with whom he came into contact. From the peaceful pastures of his native Arran to the heat of the Holy Land, from the smallest village community centre to the most famous concert hall in the world, James gave his all, whether by his robust humour or his gentle, caring hand or word. At virtually the peak of his fame, and at a point when his enormous energy seemed ceaseless, he was taken from us, leaving a vacuum which will never really be filled. It is on this overall scenario and The Scottish Fiddle Orchestra with whom he worked so closely and so generously that the overture is based.'

The piece opens with a reading of Burns's *Epitaph on my Ever Honoured Father*. It continues with music to represent James's early days in Arran, his academic studies and love of sport, particularly the 'insatiable fascination for his favourite football team.' The Currie humour, Burns, Holy Land and connection with the orchestra are encapsulated in tune. The overture reaches its own spectacular finale with a poetic tribute to the minister by Allan Ramsay and the singing of Amazing Grace and the twenty-third psalm to the tune of Crimond.

This is particularly fitting because James insisted that this should be sung at the end of every show.

John Mason is a doer. He runs two careers in tandem and still makes time for charitable works. He was awarded the MBE for raising £1 million for charity through orchestral performances. But one failure disappoints him.'

'James just loved *The Arran Shepherd*,' John said, 'and I always meant to put words to it.'

He lowers his head and is silent for a long time. What is done cannot be undone. But what is undone can be done.

He says: 'There's still time.'

James Currie enjoyed recognition such as the musical tributes of John Mason but he emphasised that he was an 'average man', and regarded this as a distinct advantage. He said, 'When I lead off a hymn it's on a key that's suitable to everyone. If I like a pop song it's sure to go high in the charts. I'm just an ordinary guy.'

Who does not, in the course of his business, employ shades of the chameleon? James's genuine self-appraisal, coupled with a childlike inquisitiveness and enthusiasm, enabled him to be himself and thus keep a golden rule, 'Never, never tell lies. They'll catch you up. If you're in a spot face up to it and that's the worst over.'

At Burns Suppers and the like Currie displayed three sides of his character; minister, entertainer and ordinary guy. At a dinner for Falkirk Young Farmers' Club, in 1973, it was the ordinary guy who spoke to Dorothy Bell, the club's secretary and daughter of a farmer in Culross, Fife. 'You Gotta Get On' was the theme of James's speech, and, Dorothy said, 'it was a simple message but it went deep into my heart and will stay there for the rest of my life.'

The following year Dorothy's father, an elder of Culross Abbey, was looking for ways of raising funds to repair its tower. Dorothy suggested a Burns Supper. James agreed to propose the Immortal Memory and helped to swell the coffers. In 1975, he spoke at another Burns Supper and, in 1976, acted as compere at a fiddlers' rally with Stirling Caledonian Strathspey and Reel Society to raise for the cash for the Abbey fabric fund.

On 17 February that year Dorothy was out with the Linlithgow and Stirlingshire Hunt. She was riding The Specialist, one of her string of showjumpers and hunters, near the Wallace Monument in Stirling when the hounds raised a wily fox which headed straight for the hills. The pack set off in hot pursuit and a huntsman urged Dorothy to keep up with them.

A happy hug for Dorothy Bell.

She said, 'The ground was new to me but my horse was fit so I kicked him on.' Then, she said, fate took a hand. 'At a disused mine, my horse skidded on a concrete slab and rolled on top of me. The saddle broke my femur and, as I fell, my riding hat came off. My foot was stuck in the stirrup and I was afraid the horse was going to run on to the road so I shouted on him to whoa! That's the last I remember about it.'

The horse panicked and kicked out to free himself. A hoof caught Dorothy on the head, splintering her skull. She was taken by ambulance to Stirling Royal Infirmary where doctors put her fractured leg in plaster but they could not treat the head injury. The same ambulance was given a police escort to the Southern General Hospital in Glasgow and neurosurgeons began a battle to save the young woman's life. Bone had entered the right side of the brain and caused haemorrhaging. The optic nerves had been severed. The surgeons explained to Dorothy's parents that her life was now in other hands. At best, she would be blind and paralysed down her left side, but the brain damage had been so severe that they cautioned she might be left a 'vegetable'. Dorothy, who was in a coma, was returned to Stirling Royal Infirmary. For sixteen days there was scarcely a sign of life. Then, on the morning of the seventeenth day, a nurse saw the young woman's lips move and heard her murmur, 'You Gotta Get On'. The words meant nothing to the nurse but when she told Dorothy's parents they knew their daughter was on the mend.

James was unaware of Dorothy's accident until he answered the telephone in his Dunlop manse and Mr Bell said, 'Thank you for saving my daughter's life.'

Dorothy had lost her sight and suffered paralysis of her left side but as she left hospital, at Easter, she sang 'There is a Green Hill Far Away'. When she got home, she asked her father to take her to the stables. There, she got out of her wheelchair and stroked The Specialist.

'It wasn't his fault. It wasn't my fault. It was just fate. But you gotta get on,' she said. Dorothy did get on, in more ways than one. Horseriding had caused her accident and horseriding helped in her recovery. Her father bought a Highland pony, 'a lazy wee thing', Dorothy said, 'but that was good because it meant I had to work hard to ride him.' The weakened tissue, muscles and tendons grew stronger from the exercise.

Andrew Stevenson, at that time physiotherapist with Dunfermline Football Club, called at the farm to help with Dorothy's physiotherapy.

That summer he explained he was going with the club on a tour of Australia but, he said, 'I expect you to be walking when I get back.' The next time he saw Dorothy she walked towards him, painfully slowly, a little unsteadily, but she walked. Later, she was to dance.

On the anniversary of the Young Farmers' Club meeting, James Currie called at Dorothy's home. 'Come on,' he said, 'I've been invited to a dinner dance and you're my partner.' James described their faltering steps round the dance floor as 'one of the biggest thrills of my life. What a girl! What a terrific, brave wee girl.'

The courage and determination which dragged Dorothy from the coma have helped her to live with her disability yet remain a fine, cheery woman. She now lives in Aberdour, where she has organised events to raise funds for guide dogs for the blind. Dorothy cannot see, but that does not prevent her from leading a full and active life. At the time of writing, she is taking a course on communications at Lauder College, Hallbeath, near Dunfermline. She still goes hunting 'although I need someone to talk me through. But my horse has more sense than me. They know when something's wrong with you and help you out.'

Dorothy would have just cause for pride in her own grit and resolution, but she dismisses any such suggestion. 'I'm so grateful to God that I'm alive,' she said. 'I was at death's door, nearly a closed book, and I've no doubts what pulled me through. It was Mr Currie's words . . . you gotta get on.'

James Currie, like all men of the cloth, was often asked to provide guidance and assistance to people in difficulties. He did not offer this lightly, but would attempt to put forward constructive assistance. He said he could do this because he was rarely confronted by a mistake he had not made himself. He was also a man who took his own advice.

One Sunday morning early in 1984 he awoke 'feeling a bit peculiar.' He was giddy and had a tingling sensation down his right side. He conducted the morning service at Laigh Kirk ('I wasn't very good') then returned to bed. He did not feel any better in the evening, but still conducted the service. Peggy urged him to go to see his doctor, but he flatly refused. His speech was fuzzy, he walked with the slightest trace of a limp, but he stubbornly continued with his hectic lifestyle, which included more than forty appearances at Burns Suppers. When he finally conceded to visit his doctor it was confirmed that he had suffered a minor stroke. With medication, his condition improved steadily but he never recovered fully. It was another warning from his body that he was finite. It was another warning that was ignored. He chose to continue working at the same hectic pace, 'You gotta get on . . .'

James saw the world as his parish and that was the fundamental reason for his popularity with the 'salt of the earth people', and what one member of the clergy described as the 'green envy of fellow ministers.' When Currie stepped over a parish boundary he trod on toes. One person grateful that he did so is a Leipzig-born woman who was caught up in the Second World War and the confusion of its aftermath.

Inge Muller was an interpreter for the British Army at its court in Hanover. She worked closely with Hugh Rutherford, a Scot in the Pay Corps, who was Captain of the Court. They fell in love and married, and Inge followed her husband to postings in Malta, Lagos and Tripoli. She longed for a baby but, after seven years of marriage, it appeared that she was to remain childless. On 19 February 1960, the couple attended a party in the Officers' Mess in Tripoli to celebrate the birth of Prince Andrew. During a particularly boisterous dance with a young captain, Inge fell and damaged her back. Her husband took her to a hospital where the doctor, Captain Baird, diagnosed a slipped disc and put Inge in plaster. However the discomfort increased and after a month she could bear it no longer.

Inge said, 'One morning I just couldn't stand it and my husband drove me to the clinic and when the plastercast was removed my tummy just came out like a balloon. I had hoped that I was expecting a child and tests showed that I was in the fourth month of pregnancy.'

Everything went well, but Inge knew that since her blood group is rheusus negative the baby might require a blood transfusion at birth. There was no blood bank in Tripoli, so she returned to stay with her husband's parents in Scotland where she gave birth to a healthy daughter whom she called Fiona. Her dream fulfilled, Inge took her daughter to Lagos, where Hugh had been posted. A year later she discovered that while she had been in Scotland having their baby her husband had been having an affair with a stewardess who had given birth to his child.

'I couldn't cope with this situation so I just packed my bags and left,' Inge said.

She returned to Scotland and stayed with her in-laws for about two years, doing odd-jobs to support her child. She divorced her husband and, in the mid 1960s, became involved in a hairdressing business. Trade was quiet, so she taught German at nightschool and rose early in the mornings to translate business documents for a London-based company.

She said, 'It was quite a tough time trying to make ends meet. I had to pay my mortgage and employ someone to look after my daughter during the day. But we were getting by.'

In 1974, Inge was the victim of a freak accident. She stood on a hairpin on the terrazza floor of her salon. 'The floor had just been washed and it was like stepping on a roller skate. My legs went up and I came down and broke my spine.' She was taken to Ayr County Hospital where once more her torso was encased in plaster. The only treatment was absolute rest, but Inge was determined that she would not be separated from her daughter. Shortly after the operation, she instructed a friend to buy a special bed and demanded to be taken home. The doctors realised that they could not dissuade her, so they ensured that the bed was suitable and strapped Inge into it. 'I had to see my daughter, to supervise her,' she said. She remained in that bed for almost a year, continuing her translating contract to earn cash. Over this difficult period the bond between mother and daughter grew even stronger. They shared joys and sorrows – and a fond admiration for a minister they had seen only on television. Daddy Currie, Fiona called him. 'Look, mum, it's Daddy Currie.'

A few years later Inge received a telephone call from Fiona's father. He was back in Scotland and wanted to see his daughter. Inge understood his feelings, and approved of a reunion, but she had always shared decisions with her daughter so she allowed Fiona to choose what she wanted to do. The girl said that her father was a stranger, and she would feel uncomfortable meeting him. Hugh accepted this and once more drifted out of their lives. However, shortly after Fiona's eighteenth birthday, she told her mother that she had reconsidered. She would get married one day and would want her father to give her away. She should get to know him. Inge did not know where her former husband was living, but she explained the situation to friends and relatives and they tried to locate him. In May 1980, the three were involved in a tearful, traumatic reunion.

Two months later Inge received a letter from her brother, a doctor in Leipzig. He explained that their father was seriously ill and urged her to come to see him. When the occupying forces carved up Germany after the war it had been decreed that she should live in East Germany. Inge Muller was a young woman who knew her own mind, and living under a communist regime was not part of her plans. She hid in the boot of a car and entered the western zone. As a punishment for "permitting her escape", her father had been sent to a labour camp for six months.'

181

After discussing the illness with Fiona, Inge decided that she would return to Leipzig. On 28 June, Fiona cooked a special dinner and the two sat chatting until midnight. Inge said, 'After just four hours' sleep I had to leave for the airport and Fiona said she would drive me. I had bought her a second-hand Fiat for her nineteenth birthday. I parked it in the driveway and tied a big ribbon and bow round the windscreen. When Fiona saw it she jumped for joy. She laughed and laughed and got in and drove it away. And she was only wearing her nightie. She drove round the streets laughing in her nightie.

'Anyway, at four o'clock I told her not to get up. I could get a taxi. She said: "Don't be silly, mum. It'll cost a fortune. I'll be fine once I get my flannel through my face".'

Inge continued: 'We had breakfast at the airport and I told Fiona – you enjoy your life; be very, very careful when you're driving home.'

As Inge was boarding an aircraft to go to see her dying father her daughter was killed in a crash.

The police found Fiona's diary which contained her father's address. He had really only known his daughter for eight weeks. He had to identify her body.

Inge said, 'I still don't know exactly what happened. Fiona took the wrong turning and was heading for Edinburgh. And she was the only one who knew where I had gone. When they got in touch with me, when they told me Fiona had been in an accident, I couldn't get a flight home. And the East German authorities wouldn't allow my brother to come with me.'

When Inge finally returned home she was distraught. A doctor gave her strong tranquilisers but sleep would not come. Friends sat with her, but she did not want them. The only one she wanted was dead. A local minister called at the house and tried to bring some comfort. Inge said, 'He brought out his Bible and just started to read from it. There was no feeling. There was nothing. He was a Bible-basher and nothing else. I was so angry, so enraged that Fiona had been taken away from me and I took it all out on this man. I told him to go away. He didn't give me any comfort. It was so artificial. I just wanted to be alone.'

Inge's friends could think of no way to console her. Then one remembered Fiona and her Daddy Currie. Perhaps the minister who had meant so much to the daughter could console the mother. He telephoned the manse in Dunlop. James was in Oberammergau, leading a party to see a Passion Play. He was just within the border of West Germany while Inge had been in the East. Peggy explained the situation and promised that James would visit Inge as soon as he could.

James Currie's schedule was hectic when he returned home on 2 July. He visited two parishioners in the Southern General Hospital; conducted the wedding service of Scottish international footballer Peter Weir in the afternoon; recorded a television appeal for Kidney Research in the evening; and then he drove to Inge's home in Prestwick.

Inge said, 'When he came through my door it was a miracle. There was Daddy Currie. He just opened those big arms wide and said, "Come to me. We will cry together." It was so natural. I didn't wonder where he came from. I just hugged him and I could feel the comfort and sincerity. He was such a big man, so big in every way.'

Currie had been asked to cross the divide into another parish. His fellow ministers would criticise him for doing so, but a woman was in need of assistance, 'How could I say no? Why should I say no?' He conducted the funeral service for Fiona at Masonhill Crematorium, outside Ayr.

He and Inge beccame great friends. She said, 'We visited hospitals to talk to children dying of cancer. It sounds cruel, but it helped me. I talked to the parents. If there's somebody else like you it helps tremendously. You don't feel completely alone. And with James you didn't have to put on a face. We comforted each other. I cried when I felt like it and laughed when I felt like it.'

James Currie promised Inge that he would find a good man for her to marry. He kept that vow and four years ago George Dunn, a Customs officer, and Inge were married in the manse at Dunlop. Inge Dunn was referred to thereafter by James as Gunga Din. George had worked hard to win his wife, and he continued to labour to secure the premises for their wedding. He cleaned Currie's study, and he has before and after photographs to prove it!

Inge spoke to me from her sick bed, where she had been confined for two weeks suffering from exhausting gastric 'flu. She smiled and she wept. I thanked her for sharing her story, and apologised for making her relive it.

'I like to talk about it,' she said. 'I have good days but then I break down and weep inside. It happens when I become happy.

When Inge's stepmother from Leipzig visited her in May of this year she found the courage to visit for the first time the Garden of Remembrance where Fiona's ashes are buried. She read the inscription she wrote eight years ago: 'When you were born I understood joy; now I know sadness.'

Many compliments were paid to James Currie. Inge's words meant most to him. She told him, 'You came into my life, you big teddybear of a man, gave me exactly what I needed.'

What she needed was a hug and someone to cry with her. Someone who understood joy and knew sadness.

184

CHAPTER SEVENTEEN

Easter Message

On Good Friday, 1987, James seized an opportunity to go back to his beloved Arran. It was a fine day in spring, one of the busiest times in the farmer's calendar. He caught the ferry at 9.45 am and, on the pier at Brodick, he met Charles, who was on his way to Iain's house at Penpont, near Dumfries. They chatted for a while then James went on to Drumadoon. At 11.30 am he fitted the plough to the tractor and set out for McClarty's Meadow at Parkhouse. Time was of the essence since wet weather had put back the ploughing by about a fortnight. He ploughed all day, turning in barley stubble, breaking for tea morning and afternoon with Betty Campbell at Meadowbank. When he returned to Drumadoon, as if to prove he had been ploughing, the rear window of the tractor was smashed. On rough ground, great caution had to be exercised to prevent the plough from jumping. There was only one way for it to jump – through the window. Currie had more time for the trammels and Clydesdales than the sophisticated adjustments required on a McCormack International 684. Four bills in as many years for windows were testament that James had had a smashing time.

After returning to the farmhouse, he took a walk up Tor Righ, the hill of the king, to examine his work from earlier in the week. The heather there had been flourishing. To keep a reasonable amount of pasture it had to be burned to allow fresh grass to grow. This was a hazardous job because there was always a risk of the fire getting out of control. The wind could change at any time, spreading flames unexpectedly or fanning embers which had appeared to be dead. This was what had happened. James, who had been burning alone, lost control of the blaze and had to call the fire brigade. It was not the first time he had been forced to do this. One of the volunteer firemen, who worked at Brodick pier, said the emergency fire bleepers went off every spring when the minister set foot on the island. The firemen arrived at Tor Righ in time to prevent the flames spreading to the shelter belt of sittca spruce James had planted across the hill some ten years earlier. About five acres of heather had been burned. The beasts of Drumadoon would be able to graze there that summer. The minister had one great regret. He said, 'The fire brigade came half an hour too soon. I could have had another couple of acres burned off.'

James could not visit Drumadoon without spending time at his wall. This was his pride and joy. The stones he had removed from the field while ploughing with his Clydesdales now formed the dry stane dyke around it. The farmer could not pass the wall without replacing a stone which had fallen: the minister would never pass a house where a soul was slipping.

Around 4.00 pm James said goodbye to Peggy who, as usual, was spending her holidays from Kelvin School working at the farm, and caught the 4.00 pm ferry to the mainland. He spent four hours travelling to have the same length of time on Arran.

That evening James took an Easter Service in Laigh Kirk. All went well, but Janet Marshall, his Sunday School superintendent, noted, 'Mr Currie seemed to stumble slightly as he went to shake hands with the members of the congregation at the door of the church and I wondered if he was all right. But when he spoke to me he sounded just the same: happy and larger than life.' As ever, there were folk back at the manse for tea. James prepared sandwiches then left them there to visit a parishioner who was ill. The guests left soon after he got back, and since there was no one at home James went to bed early, around 11.00 pm, and wrote up his diary. The final entry reads: 'What a Glorious day.'

At 4.00 am James Currie dialled 999. According to Helen Tocome, who took the emergency call, he was calm and lucid.

He said, 'I am the Revd James Currie, of Laigh Manse, Dunlop, and I am having a heart attack.'

Helen said, 'How do you know you're having a heart attack?'

He replied, 'I've had one before and I know what it's like.'

James knew that he should not try to move. The house was locked, but he gave the name and telephone number of a friend who had a key to the manse. Helen assured him that an ambulance would be there as soon as possible. She said he was calmer than she was. 'Make sure they switch off the burglar alarm,' he said.

When the ambulancemen arrived James was in pain, but appeared to be past the worst. However, in the admissions of Crosshouse Hospital his condition deteriorated. He died there, after suffering a massive heart attack.

The police telephoned Iain's house at Penpont to break the news. Peggy was spending the night at a cottage which did not have a telephone and there was no one at the farmhouse so James had given the ambulancemen Iain's number. There had been an inevitable delay before the ambulance reached the manse, so why had he not called his sons himself to say he was being taken to hospital? He had not called his own doctor, or a neighbour or a friend or a minister. Why?

Everyone who came into contact with the Revd James Currie during his last hour remarked on his composure and calmness. He not only knew what was happening but was in control. It is fair to assume, therefore, that he chose not to get in touch with anyone, not to cause worry or anxiety. I believe that he knew he was dying. He had told me that he would be happy to meet his Maker, 'I will do so with absolute confidence,' he said.

Glasgow Herald

Graeme Souness is shown into the church by Church Officer, John Gibson.

Mourners listen to the service outside Laigh Kirk, Dunlop.

Even in death, confrontation with the Church of Scotland was not ended. Members of Kilmarnock Presbytery arrived at the manse to offer condolences and assure Peggy that they would take care of all the funeral arrangements. James had died 'in harness' and protocol stated that he would be given an official Church funeral. Peggy asked for reassurance that there would be sufficient space in the kirk for friends and members of the congregation. She was not satisfied by the reply.

'Then,' she said, 'we will make the arrangements ourselves.'

This did not meet with approval. It was for the presbytery to bury its minister.

Margaret Flora McLean Currie, who describes herself as 'unsuitable as a minister's wife', was faced with a dilemma. She knew James would have hated the pomp and ceremony. He was 'a man of the people in life, and would remain so in death.' She stated firmly that her sons would take care of the arrangements. The presbytery yielded a little. There would be some space available for the members of the Laigh Kirk congregation. Then Margaret Flora McLean Currie acted most unlike a minister's wife. She told the presbytery to 'go to hell'.

The following day she instructed her lawyer to inform the presbytery of the arrangements for her husband's funeral:

1. The Revd Ian McKenzie was to deliver the main address.
2. The Revd Melville Schofield and the Revd John Weir Cook were to be involved in the church or at the crematorium.
3. The people of Dunlop would be guaranteed access to the church.
4. None of the ministers from Kilmarnock and Loudon Presbytery was to wear clerical robes.
5. The Moderator of the presbytery, in official robes, would open the service.

The family also ran into problems when they tried to make arrangements for the crematorium at Masonhill, outside Ayr. They well knew the volume of people and traffic which would descend on the crematorium and the problems which this would create, so they asked if they could reserve the last service of the day. This would ensure that mourners for a following service were not delayed and that those attending the service for James had suffcent time to leave the premises.

Charles said, 'We didn't want to delay another service, so I explained the problem and asked for the last service of the day. The

superintendent said he would try his best to help, but cautioned that if another service was requested he could not refuse. I then asked if we could book an hour, the equivalent of the last two services of the day. I said we would pay for the full hour, but was told this was not possible. I then contacted Councillor Struan Stevenson, leader of Kyle and Carrick District Council, and he told me that as far as he was aware there was nothing which in law could prevent us form booking the hour. However, when I passed on this information the situation did not change.

'I then contacted George Foulkes, MP, and after he made inquiries we were told that everything possible would be done to ensure that there was adequate time for the service to take place and the people to leave the premises.'

The family's decisions were taken after one question had been answered, 'What would James have liked?'

It is ironic that the value of a man's life is reflected by the people who attend his funeral. More than 1000 folk from all walks of life went to the small kirk on 22 April. There would have been more, but James's family gave permission to allow Westsound Radio to broadcast the funeral service as it took place. Television cameras and newspaper reporters recorded events. Policemen directed traffic as around 200 vehicles arrived in the narrow streets. The members of Laigh Kirk sat in their usual seats, other folk stood in the aisles, and about 500 hundred stood among the tombstones in the graveyard to hear the service relayed over loudspeakers.

The gathering was a cross-section of Scots society. The media reported that the mourners included about fifty ministers: the Earl of Elgin, MPs, the convener of Strathclyde Regional Council, and officials and players from Glasgow Rangers, led by chairman David Holmes and manager Graeme Souness. Currie's 'black sheep', who turned out in force from all over Scotland, never rated a mention. How much more difficult was it for them to get to Dunlop? Many of them were clad humbly, certainly not in the conservative fashion for a funeral, but they came, rubbed shoulders with the dignitaries, and everyone prayed. ('I don't care about labels . . . a man's a man for a' that.') As the cortege made its way to Masonhill, the police stopped other traffic on the Ayr by-pass to allow the funeral procession through. The car park at the crematorium was soon filled, and the approach roads lined with cars. A farmer gave police officers permission to direct drivers to one of his fields. The crematorium was filled to capacity and again mourners had to stand outside. It was an hour after the service finished before all of the cars could leave the area.

If James Currie could have chosen how to spend his final day on earth he would have altered little. He had three great loves: his Church, family and farm on Arran. The three had an equal share of his last hours. Any number of people could have been in the manse before the ambulancemen. If he couldn't have Peggy he wouldn't have anyone.

As he drew his last breath James knew it was Easter, the time of death and resurrection.